How to Epically Fail at One Planet Development

Tess Delaney

With appendices by Pete Linnell

Blue Mountain Press

Copyright © 2020 by Tess Delaney

By the same author: Horsemanship by Osmosis – A Horse Book for Non- Horsey Hoomans

Appendices - **Pete Linnell**

Cover Artwork and illustrations - **Robert Amos**

Blue Mountain Press

Printed in the UK
First Printing Edition, 2020
ISBN 9798660065354

CONTENTS

1 Great Expectations

2 The Impossible Dream

3 Homeless in Pembrokeshire

4 Carry On up the Council

5 The Moor Murderers

6 Merry Christmas, Mr George

7 Rent, Boyo

8 NoPD

9 #Je Suis Albert Dryden

10 The Enemy Within

11 And the Little One Said, Roll Over

12 Brum Brum, Let's Go!

13 The Gloves Are Off

14 Home Truths – In My Defence

15 FanDanGo

16 The Last Waltz

17 The Leveller

18 An Inspector Calls

19 The King is Dead, Long Live the King

20 Computer Says No

21 The Book of Revelation

22 And Justice for All....?

23 Charge!

24 The Show Must Go On

25 Every Cloud

Epilogue

Appendices - by Pete Linnell

INTRODUCTION

This book was written in more or less real time as my planning process took place. Some chapter parts will be recognizable if you have read my blog. Some chapters are completely new. It has been left in its real time format as much as possible and edited for clarity and flow, but apart from that, I wanted the narrative to unfold as it happened. I'd have never have got it together to write it all down after the event.

You can clearly see from the title that I failed, so this is like a play by Brecht, in that you already know the ending. But it's not a story book. It's not supposed to have you on the edge of your seat. It's just to show the process, from more or less beginning to end, for everyone who feels they want to give OPD a try.

One night I had this dream:

I was part of the crew of an aircraft carrier. Only the ship was stuck on dry land. It was still launching its jets and doing its thing, but it was marooned half a mile from the ocean. The sailors all knew how screwed up the situation was; they felt a keen and constant distress. The only bright spot there was a Marine gunnery sergeant onboard nicknamed "Largo". In the dream it seemed like the coolest name anyone could possibly have. Largo. I loved it. Largo was one of those hard-core senior noncoms like the Burt Lancaster character, Warden, in *From Here to Eternity*. The one guy on the ship who knows exactly what's going on, the tough old sarge who makes all the decisions and actually runs the show. But where was Largo? I was standing miserably by the rail when the captain came over and started talking to me. Even he was lost. It was his ship, but he didn't know how to get it off dry land. I was nervous, finding myself in conversation with the brass, and couldn't think of a thing to say. The skipper didn't seem to notice; he just turned to me casually and said, "What the hell are we gonna do, Largo?"

- Steven Pressfield, *The War of Art*

For Dan, My Folks, Lilly

To Kino and Albee, I'm sorry I never built you a house

And for those that won the game, I salute you

1 Great Expectations

The time I remember and value the most, was when me and Albee were sitting in our static, talking nonsense, in the semi-darkness, in a field in Llawhaden called Darklands.

At the time he was 14. We had sold the house in Narberth, and moved in with the horses, after reading that Charlie and Meg in the Roundhouse had finally got their planning permission under OPD. Their case had been going on for years. I was fast coming to the end of my rope after separating from my husband. The house was getting too much. I'd lost my shop and getting work had been hard. I'd been working with horses, working in shops, shoveling, shit; then my back went. Again. Then I had an accident where my back was broken. Long story. The bloke involved is dead now. It was all going horribly wrong, to say the least.

The news of Charlie and Meg scrolled its way past on Facebook – probably an article in the Telegraph. The council had been made to look right wallies. Awesome, I thought. They did it. There's an answer. Let's do it.

Kino, at this point was 23. Not a hope, Mother. He finally left home. But Albee and me budged in with the horses, and parked a caravan, and foolishly, thought that if we were honest with the council, and didn't try to sneak about, that we would be fine.

The nights were already drawing in. It was late August when we moved. We would light a bunch of tealights when it got sullen, and then, four hours later - when they ran out - it was time for bed. During winter this happened at seven pm. We didn't care. Albee was on America time, talking to chums over there online, nicking my phone when his battery ran out, and was home schooled by then. It didn't matter. Time. We were more comfy than we'd been for ages, because we hand some house funds left to live on.

By November the enforcement officer had rocked up. Our little rest was over. She was pretty nice. She explained to me nicely that I was barking up the wrong tree, but I couldn't see that; I was still in crazy mode. I nodded. I told her I was planning to do OPD. I told her we had had to sell the house and that we were getting our heads together for the mission. I told her a lot of stuff. She went away, and I kind of thought that was that.

I phoned Tao Wimbush at Lammas to get advice about doing OPD. It sounded extraordinarily complicated. My mind went numb when confronted with the hoops you had to jump through. Meanwhile, the inevitable to-ing and fro-ing was going on with my husband. You know what it's like. Splits can take a long time and a big load of drama. And that's the world I became embroiled in. OPD couldn't have been further from my thoughts. I couldn't get my head round the expense, the time, the hassle, the paperwork involved. I just didn't have the mental capacity. Just getting through the day became hard work. Albee inevitably gravitated towards his dad's more and more. World of electricity and central heating. I found myself in this place, alone, with the kids scattered, losing the plot.

Eventually of course, the council sent their letter, and their enforcement notice. I hardly noticed. The village had got an anti-hippy petition up. I hardly noticed that either until it was too late. I realised that leaving was inevitable. So I bought a bus and quickly converted it, ready for the off. I wasn't sure where I'd be going, but for a long time there had been a bit of rough land for sale, cheap, up the mountains. I could pay some debts, get a bit of land, bugger off. It was near Alb's dad's yard in Llangolman. It was close to the flat where he lived, easy for back and fore childcare. It was better. It was nice. It was wet, but it was nice. A fresh start.

The bus trundled north. Albee always said he preferred the bus to the static, as all the doors in the static were like a puzzle. My friend Jane came to help with the move. The plan had been to wander up sometime late afternoon. I was going to temporarily park on Alb's dad's field while my land purchase went through. There was no real rush, but I wanted to get a wriggle on. We ended up leaving really late, due to the fact that two of the cats had seen what was happening and refused to load themselves into the bus. They sat there, underneath, mewing, which set the others off, mewing. Eventually they all got in and we left.

When I first brought my bus to Llawhaden, the old farmer from the village, Emrys, was impressed that I got it over the bridge at Gelli.

"You won't get it the other way though, girl."

"Why not?" I said.

"Cos the angles is all wrong."

This was going through my mind as I tried to get the bus over the bridge the other way. It was dark, half ten at night. As he'd predicted, I got wedged between the two walls and that was it. Jane appeared at the door from her car following behind. "Don't press the button!" I yelled, terrified that she would open the door and all the pissed off cats would spill out into the river. I reversed back. For some reason, loads of traffic suddenly appeared. It was really embarrassing. So yeh, for ages I'd been saying, "pah... Gelli... you can get a bus through there", What I meant was just one way.

And here I was, on the point of no return, going the long way up the A40.

All was good. We were at Ken's field for 6 weeks and then my land purchase was complete. Here was another mistake. I moved my bus onto my land on a day the neighbours were home. Needless to say. They weren't impressed.

The bus was freezing, so I got a trailer caravan. Then, after watching one too many Ray Mears and the Dick Proenneke documentary, *Alone in the Wilderness*, I built the little cabin. My plan was to sit tight, see if I could get the land to work, and then apply for OPD.

But the drama followed me of course. My husband needed to move out of where he had been living, and I let him put a caravan on my land. That was another mistake.

I won't go into the ins and outs. It's irrelevant, other than it distracted me from my mission again. This is one of the things I can't seem to get the council to understand. Life has this way of messing with you. My brain ain't great. It gets foggy. I get brainstorms. I know you're not allowed to call it that now. But it's the only way I can explain. You get distracted, caught up – lost. I was very much that way. And very unable to cope. Along came the enforcement officer, again, a different one, the North Pembs one, because the holiday home neighbour next door had reported me for being here. She was all chummy right up until my husband - who was a broadband engineer and installed her broadband - left. She then turned on me. No reason to be nice anymore.

When the enforcement officer, Tony, turned up, he was nice too. Like the last one. It was only because the holiday home neighbour repeatedly reported me that they came down on me so hard. I know that now.

Once I'd been busted, I had no option but to apply for some kind of planning. I'd been avoiding OPD because it was so complicated, always assuming I'd get round to it. But now it seemed the only option.

So I called Tao.

2 THE IMPOSSIBLE DREAM

The One Planet Development scheme is a Welsh Assembly initiative that allows zero carbon homes to be built in the open countryside, with the proviso that the applicant can prove they will provide at least 65% of their basic needs from the land. This is a broad description. And it's more complicated than that, but we have here the basic premise that if you can live in a way that will be zero carbon, and mitigate as much carbon use as possible, and that you can grow your own food, cope with a compost toilet (which is usually outside) rely for heating and power on wood, wind, solar and clever use of windows, and overcome the difficulties of the limits such a life imposes, then the reward is that you get to work from home, work your land, and we see a return to the old croft system, where communities are built, land use is closely managed, journeys kept to a minimum, commute times slashed.. you get the idea.

I remember when the original article was published, because I was one of the people quoted in it. I had just been refused OPD for my site in Rhosfach, in the Maenclochog ward of North Pembrokehire. My local councillor, Huw George, had been on the BBC Wales news, telling the nation that OPD was not fit for purpose.

When I made my second application, Cllr George and I had a meeting along with some other people in order to discuss my application. He said he would help me, and in the case of a second recommendation for refusal, would insist that the case was taken to committee to be heard democratically. Last Friday I received my second recommendation for refusal, and at the time of writing I am waiting for a reply from Cllr George, having messaged him that night to ask if he is still willing to support me. He has the power to put my case in front of the planning committee, who have shown themselves largely in favour of OPD applications. This way my application would be assessed by the committee, and not just be the judged on the opinion of one delegated planning officer. In effect then, my fate lies largely in the hands of someone who is a self-professed opposer of OPD. Tricky.

So we come to our first problem. Why is it that a decision that impacts on someone' life so completely, can be taken by one delegated member of the council planning team? OPD is still in its infancy, and there are questions on both sides which need ironing out. It seems however, that the planning officers do not wish to undertake such complicated matters.

Which takes us to our next point. Why did it take five months to refuse me last time, and nearly seven months this time? The planning schedule is supposed to give you a decision with eight weeks. If they fail, they are supposed to request an extension before the deadline and ask for more time. On my first application, my planning officer was extremely late asking for an extension and then went over the new deadline anyway. The second time, I was not even asked for an extension. So of course, such a long wait has you phoning up in desperation, just to be number 500 in the queue, and then you get through and then they're "not in the office". So you email, and they ignore you. I was asked to not to contact my planning officer. I was expected to be left hanging for months on end, waiting for my life to begin and losing seasons, all while they put the OPD applications aside, and deal with easier matters.

It's not just me. Local businessman, Daniel Badham - a tree surgeon of high repute in the area, born and bred in Pembrokshire - applied for OPD on his site in Reynalton last March. That's right. Nine months ago. His planning officer has constantly fobbed him off in the same way mine has; either by pure ignorance, or by pretending that they're going to work on your application and then not doing anything of the sort. Daniel has been living away from his daughters the whole time, staying in a caravan on his dad's farm for what he thought would be about eight weeks. He's now heading into his second winter. His kids are growing into teens and losing interest in the whole idea, feeling no doubt like it's all some big lie, and they'd be right. Not a lie from their dad, a lie from the council, about how long they expect these things to take, and as to whether or not it might actually happen.

Another local chap, Stephen De-Waine, a fisherman of the Haven since he was a young man, has now sold everything he owns, including his fishing boat, and purchased a plot of land with the intention of doing OPD. "The thing that worries me" he said, "is that the council seem to be trying to stall OPD as much as they can get away with. I'm 54. I can't waste time waiting for them to make a decision if it's going to take me a year". And he has a point. Unnecessary stress is not something that will be welcome in his life. And why should it be? It's only a planning application. We're not asking to bring back hanging, although from the level of vitriolic response to applications, I'm not sure some locals wouldn't welcome such a thing.

Young people watching my progress on social media, who are thinking as they watch that this may be an opportunity they're possibly interested in, must see the agro and decide firmly not to bother. I know, given my time again, that I wouldn't. And I'm nearly at the stage where I'd say to anyone, don't do it. It's a nightmare. That's hardly a good advertisement for a Welsh Assembly policy that intends to do all it can to promote greener, more self-sufficient living.

In May 2019, PCC declared a climate emergency. Since then, they've been doing everything in their power to make the greenest policy they have as impossible as they can make it. I still have no idea why I've been recommended for refusal, as my planning officer has made a decision, but hasn't done the report yet. And I don't get this information sent to me personally; it's posted online for me to read in public along with all my objectors.

This is my third point. To apply for OPD you have to present a 50-100 page document, outlining every single detail of your plans, your life, your outgoings, everything - some of it very personal information. This information is then published online. If the council ask you a question and you answer it, they also publish that, which resulted last time in the council plastering my mental health issues all over the internet.

In Carmarthenshire, the council are much more understanding, and applicants have the advantage of being able to see the objections online. A quick gander at some of these and you begin to realise the level of prejudice we're up against. Everyone panics. "We've got hippies!" They cry. No matter who you are, they see muddy boots and recycled items and they think the brew crew have moved in. Applicants Rose and Mike Quirk, who have a site in Llangolman, have stated how alien it is for them to be perceived as such ne'er do wells. "We've always been respected before!" said Rose, who has degrees in both nursing and psychology, and Mike, a traditional timber builder. Their application is currently at the five-month mark, again, not even close to eight weeks.

So why the lies about the timescale? Why not admit that they don't have the resources and tell you you're looking at around six months, minimum for a decision? And that's a fourth point. Lies. I was told by my planning officer that I wasn't allowed to see my objections. I have since found this not to be the case. In the end, a friend put in a freedom of information request and got them for me. Why did that have to happen? I should have been able to see the objections. How come the objectors get such privacy when my life is laid bare for all to see? Objectors are usually people who have seemingly wonderful lives, but who somehow have nothing better to do than to constantly complain about everything and anything. They're the same people who used to phone up DVLA when your tax disc was a day out.

So what happens now? Well, personally, I go to appeal; a very expensive undertaking for the council, and risky for them, in that most OPDs are granted permission at appeal, which makes the whole exercise one of wasting everyone's time and money. Appeal will take 6- 8 months. If I win, the council have to pay all my costs. They say the applications are taking so long because they're under resourced, yet they can suddenly rustle up twenty grand to mess with my programme.

And then, are they're going to take Rose to Appeal? And Dan? And Steve? How many of us are they going to make an example of before they just accept that this is an assembly initiative which local council politics and nimbyism should have no part in?

OPD is capable of answering a legitimate housing and working need for many people in this county, where jobs and affordable homes are few. Farmers are having to diversify. Why shouldn't they raise a few quid for their retirement by selling a few acres to a couple of young 'uns, or not so young 'uns, to create a life for themselves, to provide themselves with jobs, a roof over their head, and be a burden to nobody, doing their bit for climate change? Indeed, there's nothing stopping farming families taking advantage of the policy, enabling them to split farms between a number of family members, and each have their own start and chance. How many farms get sold? And they never get sold to anyone local, that's for sure. My son's dad's farm in Trelech ended up split and sold. But I'm not allowed to recreate farming life with him. Why not? If OPD had existed then we could have kept a bit of his birthright for him.

When I first bought my land, I tried to find a house to rent locally. So many empty houses, not one for rent. All the little croft cottages are now holiday cottages. So where are we supposed to live?

They say - "why should hippies get away with it?" One, we're not hippies. Two, We're not getting away with anything. OPD is a route available to all. Everyone is free to buy the land, commit to living off grid, and providing for themselves. We'd all love to buy a farm, but the sad truth is, local people have no chance of buying anything more than a semi, and even then, it's tricky. I've owned houses, and worked full time to pay for them, leaving and returning to the house in the dark, dumping my kids, getting home late, freaking about childcare in the holidays... we've all done it.

It's a harder life than emptying a chamber pot, growing veg and lighting a fire that's for sure.

OPD isn't for everyone. It's not an easy life. All the more reason why the people attempting it should be supported in their attempts to create a less consumerist world, planting trees and plants for pollinating insects, growing food and being as self-sufficient as possible, on natural land, that is balanced, cared for and not smothered in pesticides. Soon it may be a lifestyle that everyone has to undertake. That's worth thinking about.

Once you get OPD, it doesn't stop there. You need to do yearly monitoring reports, and if you're not complying, or succeed as much as they want you to, then they make you take down everything you've worked for, and you've got five years to do it all - build a home, a business, and prove your worth. So much for "getting away with it".

You can't incite a revolution if you're not prepared to fight, as they say. So some of us have to be the ones to get through these early processes. Perhaps don't have the energy of the guys at Lammas, or Charlie and Meg at the Roundhouse, or Tony Wrench. That's yet to be seen. But ultimately, it's still my land. I have options. But it's pretty crazy to disallow me to make a home and living for me and my son. The real stinger is that my first refusal said that I hadn't done enough to start my business. So, I've been doing loads of set up stuff, only to be told now that they're going to refuse me. Not only that, they intend to pretty much immediately enforce my workshop, that doubles as somewhere to keep baby goats when it freezes, and is where my cats and dogs live.

And essentially, pretty soon, all homes will have to be eco homes. The council said this themselves at a meeting in May. The next LDP will contain such policies as all new builds being eco builds. I've planted hundreds of trees on my site. I've planted hundreds of trees in pots. They're growing happily on a site the council say can't grow trees. My business plan is for a tree nursery, with trees grown with local seed and cuttings, and not imported. All we see is that governments are encouraging tree planting. As ash die-back decimates our county, the council see fit to refuse an application for tree nursery. Do you understand? Because I don't.

9 HOMELESS IN PEMBROKESHIRE

After my refusal I contacted the homeless unit at Pembrokeshire County Council. A nice lady, and they can help me. As I'm responsible for my son, we can be accommodated at the hostel in Pembroke. Thing is, I used to work at the Prince's Trust, with kids that lived at the hostel, and there is no way on earth I'm taking my kid there. Not happening. And Pembroke? A forty-five minute drive from my land where I have to visit twice to day to tend my livestock. Given that one of the reasons for refusal of my OPD planning permission was too much driving, then that's a solution that seems absurd, to say the least. So now what? Luckily, having procured a gig here at your favourite local rag, I've got a few more resources available. So, let's have a look, shall we?

Looking around at the prices of properties available to rent can leave one feeling pretty bereft. What I want to know, is how does anyone afford these rents? The cheapest two bedroom I can find close to my land is in Clunderwen. It looks fabulous in the pictures, but I know it's rough, because someone I know used to live there. It's a pretty little place, with a good amount of space, but the garden is shared - which isn't mentioned in the particulars of course - and there are usually snails in the front room. The fridge has to live in a cupboard under the stairs because the kitchen isn't big enough, and there's a washing machine, but it doesn't work. My point is, anything close to affordable is slightly sketchy.

It's weird when you're renting, and you lie there in bed, looking up at someone else's peeling paint on the ceiling, unable to do anything about it because they don't want you to, and you're not really inclined to, being that your contract is at most a year long. And who in Pembs is in a position to buy? Really? Are there any first-time buyers left? And what do they buy? There's not much on the market locally for under 100k. How do people raise mortgages? Some people have to rely on parents or suchlike, but some don't have that kind of help. And there are no council houses, because they all got sold. I remember my grandad refusing to buy his council house. "They're social houses for people in need" he used to say. The next people to live there bought it. Now it's a private let, with a rent as high as any other three bed in that particular town.

I've put my name down on the council house register, because the council are basically not giving me a lot of choice. It's daft the I own and work on land that I have to leave at night times. I'm there all day. What's the big deal about where you actually sleep? Why does that constitute home? What is home? I can't be homeless, when I've got more of a potential home than someone who is actually proper homeless, but they're telling me I'm homeless. Define homelessness.

When I first bought my land, I tried to rent a house nearby. Even though there are loads of empty dilapidated properties, none are available for use. I put a shout out on the local Facebook page and got not one reply. A week or so later, someone put a post on the same page, asking for a holiday let for their family to use at Christmas. About thirty people replied, with photos of lovely little houses, that looked small enough to be affordable to a local family to rent. But they're all holiday homes. Every single one. It's no secret that many villages in our county are made up almost entirely of holiday lets and second homes. Our prices are inflating all the time, especially when bright sparks at the Daily Mail publish articles on how you can get a house in Pembs for half the price of Cornwall, so why not move to Pembs, and buy up all the housing stock? It wouldn't be so bad if the housing stock got replaced, but every time someone puts a planning application in for affordable homes, or even any homes, the vigilantes come out, insisting on keeping as big a radius as possible around them, even though they're usually people that moved here to retire, and all they're really worried about is their property prices and the feeling that any new builds will spoil their postcard. It's an endless circular mess, and to be honest, who of you, reading this, would rather take your kid to the hostel than move onto your land illegally and face court? If that's the choice, I know what I'll be doing.

I'm lucky in that my son's dad is letting me, as well as the kid, crash at his place while I look for somewhere, or get planning at appeal, whichever comes first. So ultimately, if you don't have an ex that's a brilliant dad and not only takes responsibility for the kid, but for me too, and steps in to help in this way, what do you do? If you don't have friends offering you places to stay like I've had, you have the hostel as an option, and that's it.

How can there be, as reported recently, so many homeless people wandering around Tenby that the chippy are giving out free meals? How did that happen? When did that happen? There was no homelessness back in my school days in Tenby. If there was one homeless person, they were almost a curio, like that guy who used to wander around Whitland and tragically, and almost unnoticeably, died in that fire. Now we have so many homeless that they're noticeably cold and alone in a place like "Fair and Fashionable" Tenby, relying on the kindness of the chip shop? According to the council's reasoning, I'm eligible for free chips. Perhaps I'll gather up everyone down there and let them live on the field. Always an option.

4 CARRY ON UP THE COUNCIL

Over the last few weeks, I've been learning all about the planning appeals process. It's wonderfully fun.

To go to appeal is not as easy as filling in a form. Of course not. It was bound to be as tedious and unnecessarily long winded as the application itself. The council made many points on their refusal, and so for an appeal I have had to answer every single one of these.

On going through the second refusal, point by point, it became increasingly apparent that the planning officer had missed large chunks of my application, again, which is a polite way of saying they hadn't properly read it, and most of the appeal process was therefore pointing out the pages and paragraphs in the original application that gave the information which they stated was missing.

Other points were things that were subjective assumptions, like trees can't grow on my land, even though there is a natural woodland right next door to me and all around my land in areas that haven't been heavily grazed for years, regenerating all by itself, with old willows and birches – the pioneer species - giving way to climax species such as oak and holly. I'm not entirely sure why the council assume that trees will point blank refuse to grow on my bit, barely feet away. I've also largely disproved their theory in that I've planted around 1500 trees and shrubs on my land and they're all growing bang tidy. They say my land is poor. I say I'll improve it with manure and compost. They say I can't bring compost onto the land. I say I'll use horse poo. They say the horses need to have a stone tablet with their grazing arrangements for all eternity written in hoof dust mixed with the blood of an eagle. I say that's too difficult. "Ha.. gotcha..!" they say. Tick. Refusal.

The last type of refusal points were such, that a simple phone call could have clarified each tiny point, but as the council planning officers are allergic to phones and emails, this didn't happen. Instead, the tiny reasons were added to the subjective reasons and they were added to the reasons that the planning officer forgot to read on the original management plan and application, and they all added up to a fortune for your old mate, the Pembrokeshire tax payer, who now has to foot the bill to send me to appeal.

Anyhoo. I did the appeal. I submitted. It was done. And it was good. Next day, along comes our old chum the enforcement officer, and bangs an enforcement on my workshop and goat keeping facilities. Oh, and the polytunnel, where the veg lives. Oh, and the bicycle, my green runaround. Oh, and the canoe, wot I collect the island eggs with in summer. They've also enforced agricultural items. Like the goat house. Goats are agricultural. Who the hell enforces goats? My workshop was designed and built to house bats, who have been spending the last few months taking full advantage of my hospitality. Now the enforcement officer says it will have to be replaced by a bat house. But they have a house. Yes, she said. They have to have a different house.

Just to be clear, it's absolutely unheard of for a local planning authority to put an enforcement on an application when there's an appeal in process. One has to wonder why I'm being beaten with a such a big stick.

Ok, so now we appeal the enforcement, and this is even stupider than the appeal for the decision itself. It's basically more of me saying lots of stuff that I've already said in the decision appeal. If I win the decision appeal, then the enforcement falls away automatically. So, what exactly is the point in enforcing me? All it does is slow down the process. Decision appeals take 21 weeks. Enforcement appeals take 40 weeks. As they have to run concurrently, I'm looking at least June, which really plays in my favour, if I'm honest, 'cos the place always looks blimmin' lush at that time of year. The site visit should therefore go pretty well.

The grounds for appealing the enforcement, are that the planning should have actually been granted in the first place. Councils have fallen down many times with this and OPDs. They usually lose. The expert eyes that have gone over my application, my refusal, my appeal, and my enforcement, have all given the opinion that I'll win. So what's going on? Are the politics in county hall so entrenched in picking on hippies that the climate emergency which they declared in May is being ignored? When I see a row of beautifully mature beech trees cut down to make room for a new executive home in Clunderwen, and then I get told my application isn't eco enough, frankly, that kind of pisses me off.

As usual, and as has been well documented over the years, all is not well at PCC. Corruption is rife. Every local has heard at least one back-hander story. It seems that if your face fits, or if you're willing to perform certain tricks, you can build all manner of concrete atrocities on agricultural land, or in the open countryside. Even retrospectively. And then the council say they don't have the means to enforce retrospective developments. They do if they were put up by poor people. But basic planning advice that's given to rich businessmen, by planning officers, yes, the same people who are giving me this agro, is build it, and they won't have the resources to fight it. I know.

The good thing about this appeal, is that it will be a public hearing, so my objectors will have to come and face me. More to the point, they'll have to face my mum. Think Peggy Mitchell after a stressful extended Christmas episode that centred around some drama at the Queen Vic. That's about how upset, angry and dangerous my mum is right now.

So, what do we do? It's too late for me to play the following games, but you can. And I know you all want to do what I'm trying to do, because you all keep telling me. Here's the way to do it.

There's a thing called the four-year rule. If you can get hold a of a bit of land, build a place, and live there for four years, you can then apply for a license to make it legit, and you basically have planning. The idea is that if you're low impact enough to get away with being somewhere unnoticed for four years (ten for a non-permanent structure, like a caravan) then you may as well be allowed to stay there. A lot of people round here have done that. More than you'll ever know. So, if you're struggling with the housing crisis, and you don't mind roughing it a bit, find some land, and go for it. One rule. Make sure you have no neighbours.

As Jean-Paul Sarte once said "Hell is other people..."

5 THE MOOR MURDERERS

This morning I got to my land and there was a National Parks truck parked at the top of the track. Ten minutes later, while I was feeding the goats, he came down with another truck which was towing a flail. Turns out, they're here to flail the moor.

Thing is, I had a wonderful arrangement with National Parks, and with the hill grazers, that my horses would graze that moor. We put them on the moor and within weeks they had found dry paths, made walkways, trodden down all the bracken; the moor was for the first time since I've known it, passable, walk-able and useable. Unfortunately, this didn't suit some people. They complained and complained to the grazers, to the National Parks, until eventually, reluctantly, they asked me to move my horses. I did, and over the summer, everything grew back.

Their grazing had been useful though, for those couple of months. There was loads more devil's bit scabious growing there by late summer, which was the whole point of grazing the horses there. Devils bit scabious is the main food source for the marsh fritillary butterfly, and great steps are being taken to preserve it. The moor is national parks land, who have a policy to graze their land wherever possible, to maintain the ground in as natural way as possible. Now they're down there with a flail, at the insistence of someone who insisted the horses were removed. And the cheek of it, their plan is to use the dry track that my horses discovered, and which was invisible before. I spoke to the nice guy in the van, poor bloke in the middle, confronted by me before 9am, and I told him if the flail goes to work today, then they'll be in the paper this Friday. He's gone off to speak to someone in charge. We will see. And look. They've gone. Little victory.

This was written last week, and today I met with Geraint Harries from the National Parks. We spoke at length, but it seems an arrangement for a big victory in this situation is not to be.

His main concerns, he told me, are recreation and conservation. Let's look at them separately. We've touched on conservation. By using grazing ponies the whole moor is maintained. By cutting a path instead, then one path sized area gets flailed and the rest is left to return to a state of being overrun with bracken, which stops the light hitting the ground, and makes the growth of wildflowers and the improvement of biodiversity impossible. Trees can't regenerate, because they need light to grow. Seeds hit the ground, they start to grow in the spring, and then the vegetation takes over and they die. There was hardly any scabious there before. Now there's loads. It seems that it will be allowed to die out again.

Geraint seemed to think that my point was, that I wanted to put my horses back there. I don't, because they kept being let out onto the mountain, and then it would get reported that they were out. Funny that. They weren't safe. I've moved them to pastures new, and wouldn't put them back on the moor if they paid me. So now, even though Geraint told me it would be great to have ponies grazing the moor, they're extremely unlikely to find anyone else with hardcore enough horses to do it, and so they've lost that opportunity. The thing is, as it's common land, it's not supposed to be fenced in, so by rights, it should be open, and the horses that graze the mountain would be able to just come in and graze this bit too. So why is it illegally fenced? And all the fuss about putting a bridle path to a gate which, once you go through it, you can't really get any further. Even on foot it's tricky, because it's so boggy. So where are these phantom pony riders going to go? Across the moor and back again?

The reasoning for evicting my horses, was that I didn't have grazing rights, but I was verbally given grazing rights by Dyfed Davies, who is the custodian of the land in question. Of course, once he started getting earache from complainers, he sort of had no choice but to get the parks to evict the ponios. Even though he also admitted it was good for the land. He used to graze his sheep there, but if they escaped over the bridge, people would complain, and so he stopped using the land. It's been unused ever since, and is a wild tangled mass of bracken and not much else. The horses made wonderful tracks in all directions, carefully finding the driest passages, and the moor was accessible for the first time since I've known it.

So, recreation. Geraint's other big point. You could walk for miles. Walkers began to use it. But one local couple, when taking their kids down for a wander to see the hut on the moor which the father of the little family actually helped to build, he was told by the owner of the adjacent house that it was private property and they weren't allowed to walk there. So much for recreational access. Again, the same people who are insisting that this flailing takes place, and who wanted the horses gone.

Are you seeing this theme emerging of complain, complain, complain?

The role of the National Parks is both conservation and recreation. I get that. But by flailing a bridle path, when the path was perfectly fine while there were grazing ponies there, is frankly, ridiculous. Geraint told me they're extremely limited in resources. Yet this is their priority?

I asked Dyfed for the last word on why he withdrew the grazing rights. He didn't reply. But I bet you a crisp pound note, it was because of complaining. I looked into it, and the legalities are that really, he doesn't have to allow it. He was doing me a favour essentially, and doing the land a favour too. Such a shame. And I feel bad that he was caught in the middle.

Ultimately. I tried. I tried to stop it. I tried real hard. But it's not to be. They won't do it before Christmas, apparently, so the hibernating lizards won't get crushed in their beds until the new year. I've got my work cut out, getting down there and trying to warn everyone to move. Thing is, it doesn't all turn out nice like the Fantastic Mister Fox. The lizards will get their heads squished, the devil's bit will die out, the marsh fritillary butterfly will fall in numbers again. The wildflowers will no longer grow, and the bit that the horse riders don't require for their gentile pastimes will be completely ignored, becoming a desert of bracken once more. Another perfect example of Policy over logic, of rules over common sense.

I could see in Geraint's heart he knew I was right. But he's got a job to do. This is the problem. Everyone is so besmirched in the world of having a job to do, that they ignore the climate emergency like it's not happening, and waste their limited resources on flailing land unnecessarily. The horses had done their job for them perfectly. They'd left a choice of paths to take. Now we have to make do with one, fake path, built on the blood of frogs and newts. And that my friends, it what your local National Parks are doing for you.

There was an OPD that was passed recently, not far from here, where the applicants went through hell because there was devil's bit scabious on their land. It held up their application by months, caused them loads of stress, until eventually, common sense prevailed and they came to an arrangement with NRW to be guardians of the land, and preserve the character and the flora. If a farmer had bought that land, it would have just been ploughed, and no one would have noticed. Thing is, all that fuss made about the devil's bit scabious on that bit of land, but here, barely half a mile away as the marsh fritillary butterfly flies, they're quite happy to allow their habitat to disappear. Amazing. Climate emergency?

6 MERRY CHRISTMAS, MR GEORGE

Do you remember that film, Merry Christmas Mister Lawrence? Where David Bowie gets buried up to his neck in sand at the end? The one with the brilliant theme tune? That's what dealing with planning applications feels like.

Although perhaps I shouldn't be bullying the planning officers et al quite so much. As Badger at The Pembrokeshire Herald remind us in his column last week, their lack of resources from on political high is perhaps more of a problem than I give them credit for. I do, however, think that if you have a job with that kind of power, then you should probably use your powers for good. I wonder how much they have to go against personal feelings because someone higher up the food chain has instructed them to do so? And how far up does this food chain go? Who really decides what happens?

Earlier, you may remember, I mentioned that Huw George - my local councillor - had promised in a meeting back in May that he would help me fight the dragons at the council, and assist me in my OPD quest. Again, I had been reminded of this by the same Badger piece from last week, his call to arms for people to get involved in grass roots politics and change things from the bottom up, as it's clear from last week's election result, there's not much chance of changing things from the top down. If you've been paying attention, it will be pretty obvious to you that Cllr George didn't in fact, don his cloak and/or armour and come to my rescue. But in that initial meeting he also told me of his plans to be a superhero for someone else. My friend Roger.

Roger and his good lady wife live up the road from my land in a static caravan. He is 76, she is 74. They moved onto their land in 1997 – pretty much 23 years ago. They've been there happily ever since. Some slight agro from the council, years ago, but largely left alone to get on with their farming and forestry life. Until a couple of years ago. Someone complained about them being there. And even though they had been there for so long, it had never been necessary for them to apply for a license under the ten-year rule that I referred to before. It had never been an issue. Now, all of a sudden, someone had complained, and it was an issue.

The council are aware of all sorts of breaches occurring in the countryside, but they turn a blind eye. That is, until someone complains. They are absolutely complaints led, and go around the place blinkered to everything else. So, for 20-odd years Roger had been happily chugging along with things, unaware that as soon as someone decided to be mean for the sake of being mean, then he was going to get into trouble. The council inevitably rocked up and gave him a hard time, and then they made him apply for planning permission, which they swiftly refused. The very next day, without so much as a knock on the door, an enforcement notice appeared on his gate. He had twelve months to get out. The twelve months is up this December. Yes. Now.

Huw George, back in that meeting in May, told me that at Christmas he would be going on BBC Wales, to tell the world about the atrocity being committed by the council at throwing an elderly couple out of their home of - over two decades - at Christmas. He bombasted and buffed, and assured me that not only would he help me, that he would help Roger too. I cried, as I was so grateful to him, and shook his hand, and thanked him so much. The other people at the meeting were similarly impressed with his friendly and helpful attitude, and we all happily went home for tea.

Alas, when it came to it, Huw didn't help me, and he didn't go on TV for Roger and Mrs Roger. I emailed him a couple of weeks back to ask him why he hadn't. He actually replied to that email, and didn't ignore it like all the emails I had sent him during the summer after that meeting. In his correspondence he denied saying he would help. An email war between us followed, and it crossed my mind to publish them here as a kind of Christmas nativity mini play, about keeping your word, especially if you're a man of God, and wondering why someone would get someone's hopes up, knowing that they had no intention of helping, but just wanted to sound good in front of a mixed gathering.

So it's Christmas. And where's Huw? Not on the Tele raising awareness about an elderly couple in the parish that have been royally screwed over, that's for sure. He'll be in his house, as fake as the turrets on his bay window, that reveals an ever so large, classy and upmarket Christmas tree. Joy to the world?

He'll be in his chapel in Llandissilio and perhaps elsewhere, preaching the word of God at Christmas, the charitable echoes of our Lord, worshipping He who encourages us to help those less fortunate than ourselves at this time of year. Peace and goodwill to all men. Except the slightly scruffy, old or poor ones.

He'll be driving around in one of those nice motors that are parked on his six-car driveway. A paragon of virtue, travelling around in warm comfort, spreading the good word, in a vehicle worth more second hand than Roger's static caravan. Worth more new than Roger's entire land probably. Homelessness? The poor? Do me a favour.

I'll help you. He said. Empty words. Jesus would have helped us, Huw.

But one great thing about all this, is when the wheel comes full circle, and Badger, our wonderful, literary Banksy of Pembrokeshire, encourages us to become councillors, then why not? Do it people. I'm learning all about it, and I'll let you know what I find.

In the meantime, I've already decided to stand against Huw in 2022. It's a long way away yet, but that gives me time, and I do enjoy an interesting journey.

Merry Christmas, Mister George.

7 RENT, BOYO

It's the new year, and time to try to start up again after the Christmas gap. I always feel like the days between Christmas day and new year are a little like the days between the death and the funeral. But that's not a very upbeat start to the year is it? So, lets' see what the property market has to offer.

My two big chuckles this week as regards looking for somewhere to live, have been a bungalow for the princely sum of £670 pcm and a couple of caravans, on for almost as much as a flat in town.

Firstly, the bungalow. Three bedrooms. Looks comfy enough. But who the smeg can afford that rent? If you can, could you please write in to me? Because I don't know of anyone who earns the kind of wages locally to pay this kind of rent, along with council tax, bills and all the other stuff.

So, the answer is of course, that someone gets help with their rent. We'll come back to that.

These caravans for let. We have here, someone with a big garden and a static caravan in it, which they are able to let out for money. However, if you own land that isn't a garden, you can't put a caravan on it and live there. You have to pay rent to someone with a big garden.

The person with the big garden is probably pretty well-healed to begin with. They have a place to live, plus a spare place to rent out to someone else. Same with the people doing the private lets. They have a house. And then they have another house that they can charge mad amounts of rent for, knowing that no one can afford it on a local wage, but it's ok, because the person can claim housing benefit.

So they have to go through the rigmarole of filling in forms, and putting all their personal information out there, even if they're working, so that someone can assess them, and decide if they come within the boundaries of needing help, which most people round here surely must do.

I bought my house back in the days of self-certified mortgages. But who can get a mortgage today? Three and a half times your income? Not anymore. Not around here, where most houses are over two hundred grand and most wages are under twenty. Even buying a terrace in Neyland for 100k is tricky. I owned a house, and I owned a business, a shop in Narberth, and then the business closed down, and I found myself having to sign on.

But I couldn't get help to pay the mortgage on my house, because I owned it. Basically, I could sell the house, and then the council would pay the buyer, a private landlord, the money to let me live in it. However, what they wouldn't do was give me the money to pay for it and cut out the middle man, not even for a little while I got my act together and recovered from the loss of the shop.

So then what happens, is that you're put in a position where you can never catch up again, and you get into the place where you can no longer keep your house. And now I'm looking for somewhere to rent, but the rents are all too expensive, unless I claim housing benefit, which I'm not prepared to do.

Meanwhile, I have land with a caravan on it, that I'm not allowed to stay on. Are we getting the insanity of the picture here? How do we fix this?

Even the council rent for a three-bedroom house is between four and five hundred a month. West Wales is the poorest part of Northern Europe. To pay that, most people need help. But there are also plenty of local private landlords, and plenty of empty local houses, that nobody needs or uses, and so they let them rot away. How do we explain this vast split between the haves and have nots?

One little experience from many years ago sums up a lot of things for me. My buddies and me used to do fire shows, stilt-walking, juggling workshops, back in the early nineties when juggling was cool. We did shows and workshops all over Pembs and beyond.

One time, we did a workshop in Monkton Community Hall. At the end of the day, the kids helped clear up all the stuff and put it all away. We didn't lose one ball. The following week we were at a posh hotel that I won't name. We did a big fire show, and a workshop the next day. At the end, the kids vanished, and so did quite a lot of our kit.

That always stayed with me. It's like those who already have feel that they can just take more whenever they feel like it, and they feel like they don't have to chip in. There's no sense of shared responsibility or care or respect. The kids who didn't have much were really grateful that we turned up and showed them something cool. They helped us and felt responsible for the kit. It meant something to them. We meant something to them. The other kids took us for granted. I feel like these are the kids who grow up to be landlords, who price their properties way higher than the locality can sustain, knowing full well that El Taxpayer will pick up the tab. They don't care where the money comes from, as long as it comes their way. The real benefit cheats are the private landlords, gaining more government money than actually goes on paying people JSA. Around 17 billion of government spending goes on housing benefit. It's not the poor that benefit from that money. The next biggest spend is on tax credits, topping up unfair wages. The system is broken.

And this is why the poorest part of Northern Europe is a Tory stronghold. There are systems in place that are working very well thank you. And no one wants that to change. Well, I want it to change. And I've been looking into that council election stuff that I was going on about before Christmas. More on that next week. Meanwhile, happy new year. And if you're a landlord. Sorry, not sorry.

NOPD

An article in the Tenby Observer last week highlighted the situation of yet another OPD that hasn't passed muster with the powers that be. Jim Reynolds and Lucy Lant of Penally told the Observer that they were "left frustrated" after their application to turn their farm into a One Planet Development was recommended for refusal (subject to a site visit) by PCNPA's planning case officer.

Funnily enough, no sooner had I seen the story, I popped up to Glandy Cross and ran into Rose Quirk, who I told you about earlier.

Rose and her husband Mike applied for their OPD back in June. She informed me during our garage forecourt chat that she still hadn't heard anything from their planning officer, other than platitudes and promises.

I've mentioned Dan Badham, who first applied for his OPD planning in December 2018. After a three-month validation process, the clock finally began to tick. It's still ticking, after being told two months ago that the planning officer had made her recommendation, and that it just needed to be signed off by her line manager (a process that in my recent refusal took two days).

He still doesn't know if the recommendation was for approval or refusal. They won't tell him. Meanwhile, they keep passing his case from pillar to post, first promising a decision in December, and then reneging on this, only to contact him just before they ran off for Christmas, requesting an extension until the 20th January. They also decided that now would be a good time to start asking him questions about his application.

To be honest, I'm trying to be a bit less whiney here, but it seems the universe is determined to steer me towards irritation and anger at the conduct of these people in charge of decision making.

Jim and Lucy in Penally stated in the Observer article how disappointed they are. They've spent all their resources on trying to do the right thing. They clearly feel as let down as I do by my refusal. And though I'm dealing with the council, and they're dealing with National Parks, they're the same entity when it comes to planning. It's one rule for one lot of people and another rule for the other lot, us lot, the ones who are actually trying to build sustainably and have less impact.

In contrast, the last green space in Saundersfoot is about to be built upon after gaining planning permission for a Heritage Arts Centre. Sounds lovely, until you realise it's actually 15 exclusive holiday flats and 15 retail units, probably to sell more buckets and spades and a few more imported crafts.

We're all very stressed about our planning permission nightmares, so, to cheer ourselves up, perhaps what we need to be doing is developing a plan B instead. Clearly, Pembrokeshire will let absolutely anything happen/be built, as long as its keeping some old money happy, keeping the holidaymakers happy (the rich ones – try getting planning for more statics on your small, reasonably priced site, I dare you) and keeping the façade in place that we're an up and coming, bustling and wonderful place. Don't go see the rough bits. No need, not when everything you need for your holiday on the harbour doorstep.

I remember showing a Texan fella and his highly painted wife around a cliff top property when I used to work as an estate agent. They asking price was close to a million quid. They wanted it for a holiday home. They didn't buy it though, because to get to it you had to drive past the council estate in Broadhaven. The person who built the house had got planning by some miracle. And I bet you a crisp pound note it wasn't by the miracle of sustainability promises or of having a zero-carbon footprint. Little Haven headland and not even a little wind turbine.

So, what do we do if we're refused OPD and we get refused at appeal? I'll tell you what we do. If you can't beat 'em, as they say, join 'em.

I suggest as Penally is so close to Tenby, Jim and Lucy could make a fortune by building pretend posh chalets, naming them something exclusive and building a mini golf course. They've got quite a lot of acres. I'm sure they could come up with something suitably offensive to the landscape and still have a better chance of getting planning than they seem to be getting with their OPD plans.

For Dan and his woods, I suggest a treetops and zip-wire type affair, with chalets amongst the trees, like a mini Center Parcs or Bluestone, with people being pretentious on hired bicycles.

For me and Rose and Mike, we're further north. I suggest for Rose and Mike, as they have more acres than me, that some kind of dry ski slope would be fitting, with a fake ice rink too perhaps. You'd fit a lot of holiday chalets on their land. For me, I have a nice wetland to play with, so I think I'll go for something like a scrambling course, or a quad centre, where you get to whizz around on rough terrain, and I'll specialise in yurt building workshops for disaffected city teenagers and take them for Bronte-esque explorations on the moor at full moons.

You see, the OPD business ideas of these guys are quite imaginative, but we're not being allowed to carry out these ideas. Our out of box thinking, however, could come in very useful for the plan Bs. Imagine the mischief we could plan if our lives were ruined and there was nothing left for us all but to fight fire with fire and play the ridiculous Pembrokeshire planning game? Especially as we're all getting given so much time to think.

Perhaps I'll give up on the eco thing, get myself a haircut and run off to be an MP. To be a councillor, or a parliamentary candidate for that matter, you only need ten people in your ward or constituency to vouch for you, and you can then put yourself forward.

No more compost toilets, just posh porcelain loos. No watching my journeys, just lots of spins back and forth up the M4 in some nice motor or another. No growing food, just being bought luxury nosh on expenses.

Tempting.

9 "JE SUIS ALBERT DRYDEN

My appeal date has been decided. It will be on the 18th March at the community hall in Maenclochog at 10am. If you'd come to my funeral, then come to this instead, as that will be much more productive.

Finally, there is a light at the end of the tunnel. The culmination of lots of hard work, heartbreak, ups and downs and round and rounds. OPD is, in its current form an absolute nightmare. The application process is long and arduous. The level of detail required is immense. The emotional impact of putting all you have into a mission, and then having months, if not years of waiting to get it through, of arguments, objections, form filling; it's a massively stressful thing to do. On March 18th I finally get the chance to state my case at the public hearing, a site visit will happen, (there will be cake) and then a few days later I'll get my decision.

If I fail, I'm not sure what I'll do next. Some people in this position just carry on. It becomes a case of putting more money in the machine. Like Space Invaders. Two applications and an appeal... dead, dead dead. Three lives gone. Put another coin in.

Cornerwood in Ceredigion finally achieved planning at the Crown Court last year, only to be now told they're being taken to court again. After three appeals and a court appearance already in the bag, estimates are that it has so far cost Ceredigion council somewhere in the region of 100k to fight this small group of people who want nothing more than to live and work on their own land. It was all over. Now it's starting up again. I salute the strength of the inhabitants there. They're hardcore. I'm not sure I could play that game.

Some people go to court and refuse to leave their land anyway, preferring instead to pay the fine over a long amount of time. That's not a bad option. A slow paid fine is pretty cheap rent.

But what I decide to do after that initial refusal at appeal, well, that remains to be seen. I could just keep fighting with fresh coins. I could run away to Portugal. I could go crazy.

There is that famous story of Albert Dryden from County Durham, who shot the planning officer dead when he turned up with bulldozers to knock his house down. He also shot a policeman and a news reporter. At the court hearing he was deemed sane, but having been through the process myself, I can absolutely confirm that he was anything but. He was jailed for life. He eventually died, having never been free to live life the way he wanted to, in 2018.

How is it possible to stay sane through such a process? A process we only undertake because we're trying to escape the insanity of a world where consumerism is king, and it's all about the latest sofa, toaster, or foodbank, depending on what end of the spectrum you reside. My neighbour once called me mental. Saying I must be for wanting to do this. She's right. I am mental. But not in the way she thinks. Doing what I'm doing is a good thing. Mental is paying 280k for a prefab.

I have a lot of friends who live on council estates or in overpriced private rentals in the county that say they'd love to be doing what I'm doing. That is, OPD, not being hauled over the coals by the gerontocracy.

So. Could this not be an answer to our predicaments? The housing need in Pembrokeshire is huge, the situation is dire. The housing benefit bill is enormous. It would be cheaper and a lot more sensible, when the council discuss their future LDP, to suggest that farmland near to towns or on bus routes could be purchased for the purpose of OPD villages.

Instead of being dumped in a council house, you're able to live on the land, help build your own home, learn new skills, grow your food. Kids on these sites would learn basic skills like tree identification, gardening. Taking responsibility for the land. And the biggest benefit? Many of these people are so distressed by their grey future in crappy, mouldy social housing, trapped in a benefits loop, that their depression gets the better of them. From my own mental health point of view, I know that waking up to nature and birdsong, with an itinerary of work for the day that is both rewarding and humbling, physical work, planning, things to build and use transferable skills, goes a long way to reducing the need for copious amounts of Prozac. Think of how much the NHS spends on anti-depressants. And though clearly there are real clinical needs for some drugs, in many cases, depression is manageable by lifestyle changes.

Diet changes occur naturally when you're growing veg and making soup out of what's available. Nothing is more exciting than collecting stuff from the garden for dinner, being inventive with what's in season. Nothing is more engaging than caring for chickens and collecting eggs. Or caring for other animals, whether pets and livestock. These are things that kids used to do a lot, and now they don't. 50s council houses had big gardens. It was accepted that people wanted to grow veg and have outdoor space. Now council houses are packed in as tightly as possible. How is anyone supposed to breathe? Or think? Let alone grow anything.

As communities, think of what could be achieved. Friendly environments where childcare is shared and the group contributes their different skills and learns new ones. Eco houses can be built for as little as five grand. They can be made modular to easily accommodate extra bedrooms if needed, when a new child arrives, or an elderly relative needs to be with family.

Think of the cash saved by the NHS, the fall in cases of depression, the improved mental health benefits of such a scheme, the way that families could care for elders in mixed age households with plenty of support and help. A return to the extended family model. The village model. The community model.

No housing benefit bills for single parents as they would be in a home that is already paid for. Homes would be off grid, run on solar power and wind. No electricity bills. Rainwater harvesting means no water bills. Super insulated homes mean low heating bills. The bane of peoples' lives, bills – all gone in one fell swoop. All you have to find money for is council tax and internet.

OPD has the potential to solve so many problems, not only locally, but nationally too. It needs much adjusting, but instead of fighting it, councils should be working out the best ways to utilise it.

If people are upset by people moving to Wales to do OPD, as Stephen Crabb claims, then he could help to campaign to make it possible in the rest of the UK. There's plenty of land around. It's not the Industrial Revolution anymore. We don't all need to be packed tightly into the cities. We can go back to the land we should never have left.

There are plenty of subsidies being paid out to farmers to leave their fields empty, doing nothing and contributing nothing to biodiversity. Imagine that land as gardens, allotments, comfortable, cheap and warm homes, that are built sustainably and with the future in mind - of the inhabitants above all else.

Think of the fun the kids would have. All that den building. Learning new skills. Skills that have been lost. Traditional skills. Imagine that today's game is building a real fortress in the trees, not a pretend one on Minecraft. That would work. Tell me why it wouldn't?

We need to make this a thing. How do we make this a thing? Help me make this a thing, hoomans.

10 THE ENEMY WITHIN

Been a tough day. I've been responding to the objections to my appeal. Oof. It's all online if you want to see. It's interesting from an academic point of view, for many reasons; the minutiae of planning, the psychology of people, the things that get hidden, the power of the use of language, the way to spin something with a politician's skill – it's all there. Some of the things thrown at me are in fact, true. Some of the things I'm accused of, I'm guilty of, but most of the things, I'm not. There are so many points to address that I couldn't address them all. In fact, in all honesty, I didn't even manage to read through the entire thing. My anxiety won't allow it. And therein lies the rub. The thing with mental illness, is that, because it can't be seen, you try to keep it hidden. Of course, anyone who has known me over the years knows full well that I'm a bit, well, you know.... Carrie Fisher meets Karl Pilkington...

The Marmite effect is strong in this one. Some of you reading this are going.. yay.. it's Tess from school, Brother Veg, the Stilts lady, that girl who won the weakest link... etc. Some are going.. it's that gobby cow from school.. it's that girl whose voice I always hated.. it's that girl who I tried to beat up in the Castle Inn in 1989 etc.... But reading the objections to my planning appeal application, I'm wondering – blimey. Am I really that bad?

And being a bit Carrie Pilkington.... and the stigma attached to that, I've created this tomfoolery Music Hall face that I present, in order to hide the demons that I see when I close my eyes, or to quieten the constant music that plays in my ears. I have been known to react in the most unpredictable of ways, and some people see what's behind it, and some people don't.

To the uninitiated I have for all this time preferred to leave them with the impression that I'm just an idiot, or unlikeable, or flaky. It's easier that way. But as it seems these days, we're all fighting a similar battle, in that mental health issues are on the rise at an exponential rate, then it's probably time we addressed these things.

One good thing about what's been going on this week, is that I've actually fessed up to my family and friends how difficult everything has been and how much I've been struggling. You don't want to upset or worry people so you try to get by. That's when things start to fall apart and you start to fall behind. I'd been doing a lot of that over the last few years.

But as I've been falling apart, I've been basically stalked and photographed by my neighbours the entire time. I've been feeling like I'm developing paranoid schizophrenia in co-morbidity with my other problems. Turns out, I wasn't imagining the sensation of being constantly watched. My neighbours have a list of my every move, everyone who has visited me, every journey I have made. I'm not sure what they can prove with this information, other than I have very little life, very few friends round, and sometimes don't leave my field or see anyone for a week. But instead of wondering how that's normal, they take photographs and use it to prove that I'm an imbecile, and make sure I stay homeless, because I'm spoiling their retirement or holiday home postcard.

Instead of coming over and noticing that I've been curled up with the same cat the whole time, unable to eat and picking which tree looks strong enough to take a rope, they're plotting how to end everything for me completely. They've watched me struggle, and then they've used it against me. And I know that I'm a div and I'm this and that, but surely some sort of basic human compassion isn't beyond them? Is this the same mentality of the people that set fire to homeless people in tents? Just the middle class, bought a house in the country version?

It seems I've been unfairly harsh on the planning department and the council. I had no idea what was going on behind the scenes, and it seems that they were dealing with way more than they should have had to. I can only imagine the volumes of paperwork they've had to go through. No wonder they were slow! I apologise to those concerned, especially the ones who have had to listen to me at my worst, like poor Rachel Green when she came to enforce me. She definitely got a good look at me at my lowest. In my previous dealings with her she was kind to me. And I regret my actions. I regret a lot of things I did whilst at my worst. But it's hard that when you try to make up for your failings it doesn't make any difference. When I'm right, no-one remembers, when I'm wrong, no-one forgets. Well. I was wrong. I know it. It's easier to live in denial, but my mind doesn't work that way. I wish it did.

I guess at this late stage, there's not much I can do but tell my side of the story, fess up to the way I've been struggling, accept that I've done my best at all times, and that's all I can do. Whatever is to be will be now.

If you're suffering, tell someone. I feel a million times better now that I've actually got it all out there to my family and friends. I have secured some official support, and whatever happens with my planning application, I'm pretty optimistic about the future. That might just be the Prozac. But hey. Get help. Talk to a person. Anyone. Sometimes it takes rock bottom to get you heading back up in the right direction. Our mistakes are not what define us. We can only feel a certain amount of shame and guilt before it's too much. Let it go. Be better. It'll come in the end.

11 AND THE LITTLE ONE SAID, ROLL OVER . . .

Many years ago, my brother, with malice aforethought, abandoned me to the parish and moved to Cornwall. He had to for work, so I'll kind of let him off. He bought a nice cottage in a nice village with fields in front and out back, with an uninterrupted view of Plymouth.

Now, all these years later, he's selling his place, because inevitably, developers have been making their way up the hill, and the final nail in the coffin was a broad terrace ten feet from his front window.

Houses started going up over the back, and the upstairs windows will look right down his previously very private garden. So of course, he's not particularly happy, but he knew it was coming. You can't move into a village with land in it, and expect that it will never be built upon, because that's how it works. Boundaries are drawn up on the local development plan, and all planning permission within this area will be granted, especially if it's a developer with lots of clout.

A similar thing happened in Maenclochog. Houses are to be built that no one really wanted, but Maenclochog was chosen because it had a school with dwindling numbers, two shops, and the resources to service a community. Population growth means that more houses need to be built. But where? No one wants them next door to them.

I saw a thread on Twitter where people had been saying, if you can't afford London rents, then move out of the city. Ok. But then, the people who are struggling with their rent, are the low waged service workers. Who will bring the Frappuccinos if the servers all live outside the M25?

Ultimately, the same old attitude is being displayed. People want their services, and their service workers, but they don't want to have to look at them, or live near them.

The land I bought for my OPD is agricultural land, which used to be part of around 100 acres surrounding a farmhouse. Over the years, the previous farmhouse owner pulled a great deal of blags, and managed to put two houses up without the council getting him to take them down.

After a time, they were granted a certificate of lawfulness in that they had been there for more than four years. He did, as they say, get away with it. The people who now own these houses, are the people that are now objecting to my OPD.

In the same way that my brother bought land in a village, and must expect more village to appear, these people bought agricultural land, but with no intention of using it for agriculture, and only securing themselves enough land to feel like gentry. Which means that the land around them was for sale. Someone had to buy that land. It could have been farmers, with machinery and cows and thousands of sheep, or it could be someone wanting to do OPD and have a small poly-culture farm, which, by way of Welsh Assembly Policy, is entitled to build a zero carbon dwelling from which to run the said micro farm.

The neighbours are very upset about this. Much more upset than my brother was, even though my OPD is in no way overlooking them or invading their privacy. The owner of the farmhouse stated in his objections that the land couldn't possibly accommodate another dwelling. Respectfully, my old housing estate would have fitted into his agricultural land garden with room to spare. The bit of land he plays with and mows with his toy tractor would be holding around thirty houses were it within a town or village boundary, I'm pretty sure my brother would have preferred a largely unnoticeable single dwelling with lots of biodiversity.

The sense of entitlement, to assume that living in the countryside means lots of private space, and then making as habit of complaining about local farming activities, is somewhat galling. They could have bought the surrounding land to ensure that no one else did, as a friend of mine did once. Failing that, like everyone else, they are at the mercy of the landowner who gets to decide who he sells to. And he sold to me. He knew I wanted to OPD.

But to my neighbours - farmers, people who produce their food, and staff who produce their luxuries should be seen and not heard, like the servants living in the basement in the gentrified houses of old. They need their Asda delivery man and their postman and their garage services and their log men and their oil delivery guys and their garçon up the road who they call for every job heavier than opening a bottle of wine, but they don't want them anywhere near. They want them away, to be clicked and called when convenient. They have purchased a postcard, only to find that it smells of slurry, and my God, don't they let the world know about it.

If it hadn't been for the dodgy geezer who put all these houses up without planning and then sold them for a fortune to people who knew no better, then they wouldn't be able to own these properties. If I get planning, I'll be the only one down here with legitimate planning that wasn't done on a blag. That's a thought isn't it. In this crazy status game, I think that probably elevates me to a pretty righteous position.

I'll always farm this land though. The animals aren't going anywhere. Neither is the tree nursery I've been building up. Neither am I. I'll still be here, whether I sleep here or not is irrelevant. So the point is, what do they actually achieve by stopping my planning? Not much.

In time, the boundaries will spread no doubt. And maybe in the future I'll have the opportunity to sell to a developer. You could fit a whole estate on my little four acres. We're not running out of room to house people. There's tons of room. The trick is getting past the people that would rather you went cold than spoiled their view

12 BRUM BRUM, LET'S GO

Last weekend I was in Birmingham for the launch of the Worker's Party of Britain.

I'd never been to Birmingham before, except through there on a National Express bus on the way from York back home to Tenby when I was 14, so I wasn't entirely sure what to expect. What I found surprised me. Birmingham is surprisingly pretty.

A quick walk round late on Friday night surprised me also, in that I was expecting to see homeless people in doorways everywhere. I didn't see any. By Saturday morning however, there they were. I have no idea where they spent the night. Possibly in B&Bs as part of the governments so called answer to providing shelter for the homeless, lining the pockets of yet more landlords.

Perhaps they slept somewhere out of town for safety, but still rough and in the cold. I have no idea. It's not like I've never seen homeless people before, but to see them in every third doorway was quite disconcerting. We were quite near the centre, so there were buskers, street stalls, everything you'd expect to see, though far more metropolitan than I'd expected. It hasn't always been nice cafés with outside seating though, I've been told.

On the journey into the city, as I wasn't driving (so you can't report me to the council for my carbon footprint, ok?) I was able to look around and observe. Lines of Victorian detached and semi-detached housing gave way to heights of flats, and council tenements, right next to Edwardian architecture with gated cul-de-sacs.

All classes mixed in together, within feet of each other, but delineating lines at every opportunity; we are rich, you are poor, us on this side, you on that side. We have trees and red brickwork; you have scuffled grass and concrete paths.

The daylight sideshow of people trying to sleep or collect coins, surrounded by their meagre possessions and paltry blankets, emphasised things further. We are in the lovely café; you are in the doorway of the empty boarded up shop next door.

Such juxtaposition within the constant hum of the city triggered all sorts of indignation in me, especially as I'd spent the morning listening to inspiring speeches by the likes of Joti Brar and George Galloway.

I had class war on the mind, but here was class integration, dichotomy acceptance, run of the mill ordinariness. Ignoring each other, Never the twain shall meet.

The amount of security in Tesco Express belied the friendliness of the people holding doors open for each other on the car park stairs. The view from the back of the Travelodge was of an old industrial building, which to me looked like it used to be some kind of workhouse.

The front façade concreted over with bright signs, the back side with broken windows providing homes for the magpies and their Halal fries. Like the theatre, all fronts and no backs, an old world hidden, and replaced with the Bullring and light shows and Marks and Sparks, with constant advertisements on screens using more power per day than I use in a year.

The history of the place, the workers that built it, airbrushed away, kept in the distant flats. It all seemed very reminiscent of home, and then you realise that all places are essentially the same. Our industries were farming and farming. Now they're subsidised farming, tourism, and caring for the ever-ageing population of Pembrokeshire.

70% of jobs advertised locally are for care workers. Little wonder, when again we have a national newspaper, encouraging people to move to Pembs this week.

Not South Pembs though, says the Guardian. Go to North Pembs. Much less busy, because all the grockles are down south. This, to a local like me means one thing. That pretty soon, just like Tenby spread up to Narberth and made it touristy, South Pembs is going to spread North, and the grockles will be here too, and we'll have no escape at all.

We already have villages in North Pembs where most homes are holiday homes, so let's fill the rest with retirees from elsewhere, and keep the work going for all those careers that Pembrokeshire has.

I have nothing against people moving in from away per se, but what is really annoying, is that they sometimes do the same as they do when they move to somewhere like Benidorm,. They turn all the pubs British, put their flags up and shout at everyone in their own tones.

The middle class version is to complain to the council about local activity, insist that farmers don't leave mud on the road, demanding the pot holes by their property are fixed and tarmacked immediately, and kick off about how slowly everything is happening for them, when they campaigned for their own private bridle track and it hasn't yet happened.

Meanwhile, there is no industry and no work. The docks became marinas. Unless you can get into Valero or the LNG sites, which you won't because most of their workers come from away, another reason our rents are so high.

It became so clear to me on Saturday, that the old class attitudes haven't gone anywhere. It's still the same old fight as it ever was, the only difference is that the class thing has been lost in the identity politics of neo-liberalism, and we're all so busy thinking about all the wrong things, and worrying our little heads about Love Island, Rights for all, PC versus non PC, Brexit arguments, that real life has been forgotten.

The loneliness was the thing that struck me the most about the homeless people that I saw in Brum that day. And it was also what I saw in a lot of the people at the rally, including myself, all looking for something to believe in, and it was an irony not lost on me that the rally just happened to take place in a church, and there's George Galloway orating like a fedora wearing king with a massive crucifix behind him.

I'm no religious believer, but I'm a believer in higher powers of some kind. The rally felt comfortable, like an old coat of people that I felt I'd met before, made up of leavers, remainers, left wing, right wing, no wing, ex-Communist party members, ex-UKIP members, ex-Labour members... everyone was represented. Many people spoke passionately and knowledgeably. It was the most inspired I've ever felt about politics.

We heard the truth about the NHS from Dr Ranjeet Brar, a surgeon, and Dr Bob Gill, a GP, harbingers of shocking truths. We also heard from working class poet Christopher McGlade, who had been getting abuse that morning on Twitter just for agreeing to turn up. Someone must be worried.

So many people have never voted because they see no point, because the parties are all the same. In that case, it's time to get involved. It's time to become the parties. And it doesn't matter what party. Just get busy. Local elections are only two years away....

Being British, we're not likely to set light to ourselves and fight the police like the French have been. But we're very likely to read something, see something, get disgruntled with the injustice and write in to complain.

Let's concentrate on complaining about the stuff that matters. The homeless, foodbank collections, the destruction of the NHS. Get incensed all you like, but get angry about things other than the fact that Pembrokeshire doesn't yet have a Waitrose and you miss it.

Try compassion. Think about the people in this county, the poorest area in Northern Europe, the people whose county you are moving to. Respect that their industries have been destroyed, and that's why you're able to buy a "cheap" house here. Don't complain about the farmers. Support them. Don't judge the people who don't have much. Understand them.

Otherwise, if all you want to do is recreate your city and push the nastiness backstage, there are other places probably more suitable.

Try Benidorm.

19 THE GLOVES ARE OFF

I got all the info from Freedom of Information the other day regarding the third-party comments for my planning permission. This means I have to go reading this stuff again and it gets kind of upsetting.

It's all very similar to the objections on my appeal that are all out there for all to see in the public domain on the planning inspectorate website, so not much new shock to be had there. But one thing that is new is that I see my planning officer was getting very chummy with my neighbours, which is incredible, because for the entire process I couldn't get her to once reply to me.

When the neighbours cut my water pipes, and I had to get my solicitor to get me access to fix it, the neighbour who called me mental also said to me that I would never get planning permission. Now I know why she sounded so sure. They had clearly already decided, somewhere along the line, in a process that may or may not have included certain sweeteners, that I was going to be refused.

In fact, my neighbours were even told I was to be enforced before I was told. My planning officer encouraged the neighbours to keep taking their pictures and sending them in.

The holiday home neighbour, who I won't name, we'll call her Katie Hopkins, because that's who she looks like, has taken so many photos of my plot that she could open a gallery. The other neighbour, we'll call her Anne Widdecome, seems to have mastered the art of dealing with the council. She's the one who called me mental and told me I wouldn't get planning.

Funnily enough though, she built a block of four stables with a concrete base with no planning permission and no consultation with NRW on agricultural land. When she was eventually forced to apply for planning, she got it, retrospectively in seven short weeks. Really?

Any horse owner in Pembs will rejoice at this, and I suggest you all go out and build those stables and field shelters that you've been thinking you're not allowed to have. You can have whatever you like. You just have to put down a concrete base, put in electricity and water and a pretentious clock, and Hey Presto, retrospective planning granted. Any issues, and I'll give you the address so you can state the precedent. Seems incredible that all these Pembrokeshire people have been making do with shelters on skids and hedgerows for all this time and all it took was a divorcee from Cardiff to come down and open the door.

PCC refused another OPD planning last week – one just up the road from here. They're going to appeal. So that's another appeal to pay for taxpayers. That's two just on this road. Around 40k is a good estimate of price for the two of us. And there are still two OPDs pending locally, which are dragging on.

The council say they're short on staff and resources, but what seems to be happening is that instead of doing what they're supposed to be doing, they're working hard behind the scenes to ensure that OPD never goes any further. They're in cahoots with neighbours, encouraging bullying and stalking behaviour.

My planning officer wrote emails to my neighbours thanking them profusely for photos, because it meant she didn't have to bother doing her job and coming on site visits or talking to me or emailing me or replying to me. She got my neighbours to do all her dirty work and then refused me, safe in the knowledge that though I'm homeless, she's got a nice big farm to inherit, and she will never know what it's like to have to get anywhere in the world herself, because she's old money and will always have all the land and farm she wants given to her on a plate.

Why are people like this in these jobs? Why is someone with no understanding of what it means to have to make your own way, employed in a job that needs a bit of human understanding and compassion? I told my planning officer about how anxious everything was making me, so what does she do? She creeps around behind my back making me feel like I'm being constantly watched. I WAS being constantly watched, at her request.

How is this allowed? Why is my enforcement information being given to other people first? Why is she replying to their emails and chatting at length to them on the phone, yet she didn't return one phone call to me, didn't reply to one email, didn't keep me informed in any way.

This is just another example of how the council are a law unto themselves, corrupt to the core. There's way much more to this that meets the eye. And I will make sure I find out every single fact, if it's the last thing I do.

Even if I don't get my planning, I will make sure that no one else has to endure the stalking and crazy-making behaviours of neighbours encouraged by planning officers.

I'm not the only one. As I dig around, I'm finding more and more evidence for underhand activity, bullying and ruthless cavorting with objectors being used against applicants. And bit by bit, I'll expose the bloody lot. Like OPD isn't hard enough, without being a single woman in a rural area surrounded by NIMBYs who think - who KNOW - that the council are on their side.

It's like a scene from Hot Fuzz. They're all in it together. For the greater good? Their accusations are even more than mental. I tether my goats? Nope.. I don't even tether my horses. And I have a holding number. And my cats are neutered. And the pest control is the cats, you numbskulls.

And what about the scrapyard next door that none of you seem to notice with the bus and the engines and the squatter? And predators to my ducks? It's your dogs that killed my ducks! I have photos! And how are you on my private Facebook page? Private account? Or fake profile? How bored are you all? I'd get you all a jigsaw each, but you'd probably only be interested if it had a picture of me on it.

So, now you all have your research degrees on Tess Delaney, what are you gonna use them for? You gonna teach a class on Tess Delaney? Mastermind? Specialist subject, Tess Delaney?

And you call me mental...

14 HOME TRUTHS - IN MY DEFENCE

I must admit that I did not manage to read all of the objections presented, as the process was too stressful. My objectors are correct on many counts. There were many problems when I first got the the site.

I got it into my head that sheep would be a good idea. Clearly, they weren't. As I had learned to use a spinning wheel, I had romantic notions of spinning their wool and using it to make rugs as part of a potential OPD idea. They were Herdwick breed, originating in Cumbria and hardy enough for this landscape. I had read their wool was good for carpeting. I'd also read that they were good at staying put in their field, unlike Welsh sheep. What I didn't realise was that their homing instinct was indeed so strong, that they would first attempt to return to Cumbria first.

They escaped many times, and I was as sick of my sheep as my neighbours were. They left the site in October 2018 (the sheep, not the neighbours). So, though I know they caused my neighbours problems, which I offered to pay for, I sorted the problem by getting rid of the sheep. The neighbours at that time were in nice mode, and didn't accept the offers. The complaints about sheep started six months after the problem occurred and coincided with my planning application going in. Then demands for compensation for sheep damage began to appear. I became defiant and thought that if it could take six months to complain, then I should take six months to pay. The police then told me I was not liable, as there were other sheep in the property at the time from on the mountain, and they had no proof whose sheep it was. They also told me that the owners should be told to fence out straying animals, if they are going to buy houses next to farmland. I did intend to pay, but then my neighbours upped their bullying so much I decided not to. I should have been the bigger man and given them the £45 they were demanding.

One neighbour, the one in the holiday home, we'll call her Katie Hopkins, had brought her granddaughter round to see the lambs. I now know this was a ruse to get my then husband to install her internet. The first time I met MS

Hopkins was when she came onto my land and screamed at me. This was in September 2017. I had been around the land since January of the same year when my land purchase was agreed. The fact that she didn't see me until September surely demonstrates that she doesn't actually live at Wern as she states. She lives in a village called Wilton, near Marlborough. I know this because when her dogs were consistently coming onto my land, I was able to get her postcode from their collars.

Katie and Anne Widdecombe's dogs came in together one day and chased and killed my nesting duck, who had been sitting her eggs for a month, losing me 13 chicks too.

I have a younger dog now to guard the ducks and geese, and she is extremely good at staying on my land. I can't take her with me when I crash somewhere else, so have no choice but to leave her behind. I don't like to lock her in to a building when I'm not on site as my neighbours have proved themselves to be not only obsessive, but I believe, dangerously so. I worry about finding my animals charred to a crisp in a burned-out workshop or caravan one morning.

The neighbours proper turned on me when I finally applied for OPD. The night my application papers went up, Hopkins sent me a series of drunken vile messages via Facebook and I was forced to block her. They clearly have spies on my Facebook, which I treat as my friends in the pub, where we chat away. People are not supposed to be constantly and obsessively eavesdropping. How is she constantly screen-shotting my stuff? Who is her spy?

When she goes back to Wiltshire, she leaves her rubbish at the top of the track and this gets pulled out for ten days by foxes until the rubbish men arrive. I have no idea why she so vehemently pretends to live at Wern. She has only been coming down so often since I applied for planning to spy on me. That much is clear. Before that she came down a few weekends a year.

The house she owns and the house that Anne Widdecome owns, were both built without planning permission by the previous owner of the land. Katie Hopkins is extremely proud of this fact and told me how they used clay from the soil to point the stones, so that testing would show that the mortar wasn't new. The farm opposite reported the building, but it was somehow allowed to stay.

Anne Widdicombe's house was a shed which got converted into a bungalow. Last year, she built four stables without planning permission and was forced to apply retrospectively. Planning was approved, even though there were no drawings provided with the application and the entire building has a concrete base. Tons of concrete were brought down the track. Many truckloads of stone and rab. All the machinery was brought down the bridle path on massive tractors with trailers, so it amuses me to see that I am responsible for destroying the track in my Vauxhall Vectra. Anne Widdecombe insisted I dig up the track to fix a hole that she blamed me for. So, I did, and I paid for it. They now complain that this work is what messed up the track as a new pipe had to be put in. The track was cobbled together badly for access to the two illegally built houses further down. It was never meant to accommodate Widdecombe's building crew and her horse box going up and down it constantly. I've since fixed this track at my own expense, only for it to become the new race track to for the endless delivery drivers that go down to Hopkins and Widdecombe's.

When I first got to the land, everyone hated each other. Now they've found a common enemy it seems they have all made friends. Widdicombe called – we'll call him Mr Bean, the farmhouse owning architect - "all the gear, no idea" and called his girlfriend – who I shall refer to as Mr Bean's Teddy - a "shit stirrer". Katie Hopkins laughed about how much it upset Mr Bean that she left her rubbish at the top of the road, mocking him because he used to put her wine bottle box down near her house, as otherwise it would sit at the top of the track for months until she came back from her actual real home in Marlborough.

I have never denied to the council that I lived at the land. I came to the land in the middle of an extremely stressful divorce. My then husband ended up following me up to the land and against my better judgement I let him put a caravan on site. There were actually two caravans at that time. We were not living together and were not together, although there had been talk of reconciliation. I'd sold my house when we spilt up in 2015. We both suffered a lot of emotional stress at that time and didn't deal with it well. I stayed with him in Crundale for a while before buying the land at Wern. Our differences meant that I ended up moving to my land to get away. He then lost his place in Crundale and turned up at Wern. He was/is a n alcoholic, and there were many fights when I asked him to leave. But when he was around, he got on ok with Katie Hopkins and she would ply him with drink when he went down at weekends to do her installation as that was the only time she was available, one weekend every few months. He went above and beyond the call of duty to install and maintain their internet which because of the position of the house was a difficult installation.

When I contacted Hopkins to tell her that I had a restraining order against him and that she would need to get a different engineer, she turned on me. I have all the personal messages. They weren't pretty, and she was clearly very drunk whilst writing them.

Mr Bean has always been pleasant to me and I wasn't aware that he and his girlfriend from Salisbury felt quite so strongly. I see now that his visits were again, false, and designed to glean information. He told my husband that he liked the cats being around because he had mice in his Lotus which he keeps in one of his sheds, and that they'd been chewing the upholstery. He then went and got himself two cats. He told me last weekend that he'd got two more because the others had disappeared. I informed him that one of them was actually living in the shed with my guys. I have 11 cats and they're all neutered. Darwin himself said that we need more spinsters in the countryside with their cats, because cats eats the mice and rats, and mice and rats eat the bird's eggs. I have to take offence to the blame for the lack of birds. 11 cats is not excessive in such a vast area. If it was, why did Mr Bean get himself four more cats? Surely, I have enough to go round? There are huge amounts of birds at my place, including a pet woodpecker that's really tame. The cats very rarely catch a bird. Last summer, Bean used his mini tractor to cut the brambles and regenerated trees in the field in front of his house, around an acre in size. As this was done right in the middle of nesting season, I suggest that there might be the clue as to where his birds went. The building of Anne Widdecome's stables also caused massive upheaval. All those works were also done during nesting season.

Katie Hopkin's partner, the man with not enough personality for me to find a fun name for, made comments that came as a surprise, in that when I first got to Wern, he also told me that their house didn't have planning permission. Mr Noname is very rarely in Pembrokeshire. He told me when I first met him that he admired Napoleon, the guy who lives in buses up the track, because he lives a free life. And this is the bit that confuses me the most. The site visit on appeal day will show clearly, that next door to my land there is a scrapyard, with buses, trucks, engines, endless use of generators, etc etc. I don't understand why the neighbours are so pinickety with my temporary washing line and those pallets I left around, but they completely ignore Napolean and his scrapyard. My place has had its moments of looking scruffy, but I'm making daily inroads into making it look good and be productive. However, the place next door gets tons more concrete dumped on it, and more vehicles and caravans, and no one bats an eyelid. This shows that in the main, the comments and objections are personal, in that it wouldn't matter what

I did, they would object. They're even objecting to the improvements I'm making, accusing me of trying too hard. When I wasn't trying hard enough?

Big talk is made of my animals escaping. Yet I had to call the police on numerous occasions for my horses being let out. I wasn't fly grazing the moor, I had an agreement with National Parks, which my neighbours complained about until I had to move the horses. I then rented the land behind mine, which dues to all the rain turned out to be too wet. They're now on permanent grazing elsewhere, and have not been moved temporarily.

When getting my grazing arrangement messed up, the neighbours mithered NRW, National Parks, the Council and the Grazing association, even though all these bodies liked the horses being on the land and wanted them there. The complaints were so much that they got sick of the hassle and regretfully asked me to move the horses. Katie Hopkins then attempted to mess up my new grazing arrangement by contacting my new landlord and telling him lies about me. She then went to the house next door, as I'd had grazing there before with the previous owner who died last

Christmas eve, and the new owners offered me the grazing back, so Hopkins went down to "introduce herself". She never introduced herself to the elderly guy who lived there before and who would have enjoyed the company. Now they're angry because they have no way of messing up my current arrangement.

The tree I felled was on the advice of a qualified tree surgeon, none other than our old buddy Dan Badham, and the work was carried out professionally by him. The tree had stage three ash die back and needed to be felled as it was a hazard to the phone lines for the neighbouring houses and to the track. This is where we see a little knowledge is dangerous, as my neighbours are so obsessed with that one tree and what I did with it, that they have failed to assess their own trees along the bridleway which are causing significant hazards and are a risk to life. Perhaps people should get their own houses in order?

I can understand Mr Bean's's point about the building at Wern since he's been there, but I don't think I should be held responsible for his inability to fight the builders of those structures with the same gusto he's displaying here. Perhaps a woman is easier to fight.

I am glad the neighbours noticed the genius of my Steptoe bathtub, which they stole photos of from my Facebook page and tried to use it as a reason to refuse my planning. For my bad back I sometimes have to improvise. Metal bath, fire underneath. Sorted.

I had things on the honesty stall at Nick's by the bridge, but had to move them because they were getting kicked over. Graffiti appeared about me in Llangolman, massive letters that say "Tess D – Council Snitch", obviously painted by the lovely and classy Napolean, as he was screaming at me on the track a few weeks later after blocking my car, that I was a f***ing snitch, a word I haven't heard since about 1983. Clearly all this vitriol and venom and all this spying and obsessive behaviour is related.

Hopkins appears to be filming me, and appears to have a fake Facebook account that she uses to stalk me. The police have deemed her behaviour harassment and anti-social. However, as her accusations are connected to a planning application, the law says that's ok. Whichever way the decision goes, this situation will no longer be the case after the March hearing, and I hope that the bullying will subside. I'm not sure Anne Widdecombe will ever stop giving me dirty looks and stopping her car to stare at me every time she passes. But I am not 15, and I do not respond to this obvious attempt at getting my negative attention.

Mr Bean's girlfriend from Salisbury, Teddy, who I have only ever seen twice, says that if I get OPD lots of people will move to Pembrokeshire to do OPD. They already are. There are four more coming up in the local area alone. However, what it has to do with her I don't know. She lives in fecking Salisbury.

I have studied horticulture for 25 years. For the last five I have studied silviculture and permaculture. The space I have now has given me opportunities to experiment. Gardening is not buying stuff from the garden centre and then saying it doesn't grow because the land is rubbish. All land is improvable. All soil can be grown upon. If trees can't be grown on my land, why have the fields next door regenerated themselves so quickly? A neighbour who likes me told me that the existing woodland was just field 15 years ago. Now it's a thriving willow area, with regeneration of climax species occurring naturally, oak, holly, growing among the birch. Woodland will grow on any land. My boyfriend complains that the tress we purchased at the same time from the same place grow better on my land than on his. On the question of numbers, biofuel willow can be grown commercially at the rate of 50,000 stems per hectare. I certainly don't need to be doing that.

When Anne Widdecombe made me dig up the track to fix the hole, I said I was afraid to tell Katie Hopkins as I was afraid of her. Widdicombe said she would tell her because she said Hopkins was afraid of her. Widdicombe used to tell me that Hopkins and Noname kept inviting her over but she didn't want to go because Hopkins was "a formidable woman". Noname and Napoleon both warned me about Hopkins before I met her and told me I would have trouble from her. That's the review she gets from her partner and her friend. But I didn't realise she would be quite so intense. It's hard to imagine that someone could own such a wonderful holiday home, yet spend all their time here bullying the girl next door. Is that really the most fun to be had in Pembs? We have some fabulous beaches...

much too boggy. I wonder if Dyfed is prepared to let a whole group of horses use his land? Time will tell. The gates to his land are not bridle path gates and are all tied up with twine. Not many horse riders will be keen on that.

These are people that do not practice what they preach. Mr Bean has every light on in his house all the time. Anne Widdecombe drives to the postbox and uses a quad to move around her land. Hopkins and Noname, when they come down, use separate vehicles. They're back and forward to Marlborough. They also have a wide selection of family visiting and staying with them. Mr Bean and his Teddy go up and down the M4 to and from Salisbury to visit each other. I am being criticised for not doing enough by people who aren't doing anything at all. My occasional use of a chainsaw and strimmer is nothing compared to their constant use of power garden tools. Hopkins and Noname spend their whole time here strimming everything to within an inch of its life. Widdecombe and Hopkins spend lots of time with hedge cutters cutting down brambles so that they don't scratch their vehicles. Mr Bean mows his new massive lawn with a baby tractor. Widdecombe goes up and down in horse lorry with her show ponies. Napoleon runs a generator and spends his time fixing and playing with large vehicles with bad engines, running them for hours. They insisted on installing the most hideous fence on the bridge that was illegally built over to the moor. And that was installed wrongly and creates a hazard for any horse trying to cross.

To me OPD is about collecting using recycled things, but they think it's all about looking like you've been to B&Q. The people come from the city and want to make farmland look like the city does. Widdecombe made the council re-tarmac the road at the top. She complains constantly when farmers leave mud on the road. She even complained about a street light on the mountain spoiling her view and wanted it switched off. I've been replacing all my recycled fence with brand new fence. Which looks much nicer yes, but it isn't OPD.

I've made lots of mistakes. I'm not going to deny that. I've been trying to make up for all of the mistakes I made, but it seems that's not permitted. I need a home, and I want to live in a simple and sustainable and low impact way in the county I grew up in. I am being halted by people who have moved here from away, all except one of whom own second homes. Mr Bean somehow managed to turn one of his sheds into a residential property that he rents out. It's basically impossible to do that in Pembs. You can get planning for holiday cottages, but not for extra homes. Not unless you've got extremely good contacts. I suspect Anne Widdecombe's unprecedented permission for stables was granted by the use of similar contacts. As is often the case in Pembrokeshire regarding planning matters, it's all about who you know.

Hopefully the site visit will clear up all the questions. The site is improving daily. I'm being judged for not having it all together, but I haven't even got planning yet. I've been doing my best, and sometimes that's been an epic fail. No excuses for that. It's just sometimes I lose strength. But other times, I'm ridiculously strong, and that's when stuff gets done. The whole process has been one of the worst in my life, but I believe in the land. I also sometimes believe in myself.

15 FANDANGO

Some good news for a change. Regular readers will remember Dan Badham, our local tree surgeon who applied for OPD 16 months ago. Today, after a committee meeting at County Hall he was unanimously granted permission to go ahead with his project. I watched the meeting online and was struck by a number of things.

A couple of the elected planning committee seemed to have no idea what OPD is or how it works. Am I mistaken in assuming they're supposed to read the agenda prior to the meeting an to familiarise themselves with each case presented, so that they can come to an informed decision? You could tell who had done their homework because they didn't have to ask any questions.

Some of the questions asked and points raised merely served to demonstrate just how unprepared some of these councillors actually were. One commented on the trees on the site, seemingly upset that they would not be managed properly, whereas if he had passed even a cursory eye over the application, he would have known that Mr Badham is a tree surgeon of some local repute. Luckily, Cllr Jacob Williams in the chair had been paying attention, and was cynically able to put the councillor straight. But what if he hadn't? At the very least, that could well have caused yet another delay in a day of hold ups and difficulties, all seemingly brought on by the fact that not all of the councillors were familiar with any of the cases. I only watched three, including Dan's. That was enough. But I've watch many of these planning meetings, and it's always the same.

Another couple of councillors seemed extremely upset that even though the usual OPD application is all tin and turf rooves, that this application actually looked like a house. I was lost at this point. Sorry, but did you mean you prefer the tin and turf? Would you have preferred a hobbit house application? He began the sentence like he was going to say one thing, and ended up saying completely the opposite.

If I was a planning officer, my first thought would have been, why can't the applicant just have normal planning permission, due to the fact that his site is clearly within the village boundary, as demonstrated on the ariel view photographs? There's a whole village right next door, a farm to the North, and a girt caravan site over the road. Sorry, but why was this case complicated?

One thing I noticed during proceedings, was that the site visit was undertaken at the beginning of the process. A letter was sent to Dan asking for permission to access the site. The photos that appeared at the meeting however, were clearly taken a good few months after that. No permission was requested for this visit. But they'd obviously climbed the gate to take their photos...

The time taken was also justified by the fact that OPD applications by their very nature are complicated. However, the committee also hear a case about a housing estate in Stepaside, which presumably was sorted within the allocated eight weeks? Why is Dan's very excellent management plan more complicated than a site where work has already started and flooded the adjacent area, with mains services involved, school crossing issues, flooding issues and all the other problems associated with such an application?

Is that really an eight-week job, whereas a single dwelling is deemed complicated enough to take a year and a third? Interestingly, the planning officer had recommended that housing development for approval, notwithstanding naughty behaviour by the developer who seems to have cause all sorts of environmental and social problems. After that, a caravan with a hot tub, concreted down and made permanent, and applied for retrospectively for holiday use was also recommended for approval, whereas my OPD was refused. Interesting.

The One Planet Council run courses for council employees and many Local Authorities have taken advantage of this. But not Pembrokeshire. Why not? Why use the excuse that OPD is complicated when you've got the chance to go and learn about it but you decline?

One councillor questioned whether the constant practice of going over time with decisions for OPD was showing PCC in a bad light, to which Mr Popperwell replied that extension requests are made and so they don't get into trouble. That's not actually true. Extension requests have consistently been requested late; way after the time they were supposed to be requested. In many cases, months after. Nearly every OPD in the system over the last year has had this problem. I had this problem and so did Dan. On my second application an extension request wasn't made at all.

Next week, the 18th March at 10am in Maenclochog community hall, is my appeal. It's looking to be quite fun. Lots of people are coming, and everyone is invited. At the moment I'm not freaking out too much. There's no point worrying about not being successful, because then I'll have suffered twice. I'm quite surprised how calm I am, although I'll probably be unable to stand from about tea -time on Tuesday onwards.

If I win, it will be a triumph of common sense over adversity. If I lose, then, well.... we'll see. I was only this morning told that I won't get a decision straight away, and it could take up to six weeks. Sigh. Put the kettle on Baldrick....

16 THE LAST WALTZ

It's with no small sense of irony that I find myself sitting and writing what I wanted to say instead of having the opportunity to address the council and my objectors in person today, due to Covid-19. Yes. Cancelled. Last minute, literally the day before. I didn't know whether to laugh or cry, so I laughed.

It was to be argued this morning that I should not be permitted to live in an isolated way and be self-sufficient, as the world collapses around us, the capitalist system is teetering on a precipice and we're facing an enormous crisis worldwide.

However, for me, nothing has really changed. If I didn't have Twitter and Facebook, I'd be unaware completely of the emerging pandemic. I shop locally and the village shops have their usual stocks of items. I have a garden full of food growing as we face mass shortages. I have a spring with water from the mountain that isn't controlled by any company or infrastructure. I have solar panels so I will have power when the cuts begin. In short, I have everything I need to hunker down and exist and live and continue with my life.

The people who are telling me that I should not be doing this are now being forced to suddenly change their entire lifestyle. They don't have access to food in their gardens, most of my objectors will be quarantined to England and unable to visit the area, that is, if they could get the fuel. This mad time in history only serves to demonstrate that projects such as OPD and similar, are the only real option of the future.

Society as it is cannot be sustained. The economy is collapsing, assets are collapsing, infrastructure and globalism is collapsing, all in front of our very eyes, in the very same week that I'm fighting for my life, literally, it would seem.

All I have is my land. I have the opportunity to create a home and a business, for myself and eventually my sons. I am no burden to anyone. I do not have to rely on an uncertain work or job future. I don't have to rely on benefits or social housing. I'm not using taxpayer's money to line the pockets of a landlord. The state does not have to care for me. If I am refused planning and enforced, I become homeless, I lose my employment, I lose future business, and the locality loses an opportunity to benefit from my project.

I want to grow the much needed trees we need to restock the gaps that will be left by ash die back, which incidentally, was brought in on cheap imported trees from abroad and distributed by organisations such as the Woodland Trust as part of their free tree scheme, where you receive a few months old barely rooted sapling about five inches high, wrapped in its own plastic and delivered in its own box over many miles to the customer.

There were five tree surgeons due to attend the meeting today. All were to give evidence that in their opinions I should be positively encouraged and supported in my plans for a tree nursery.

There is no arguing that there is a climate crisis, whether man made or natural is irrelevant. We need to stop doing what we're doing. The last few days fundamentally demonstrates this. The sky is clear of aeroplane contrails. The waters of Venice are running clear and fish and dolphins are visible. The world is recovering really quickly. If this lockdown became the new way to do things, the planet would improve, whether natural forces are at play or not.

By consuming less and providing for ourselves, we're at least giving ourselves a chance. The world is changing exponentially. Something has to change. This new situation that we find ourselves in will dictate the pace. Pretty soon we'll all HAVE to do OPD, or something very much like it. We'll have no choice.

From a personal point of view, this whole process has felt like I'm begging for my human rights. Until the meeting was cancelled, I felt like I was on Death Row.

We're a local family. My sons were born in Withybush, as was my grandaughter. Something that we will not be able to say for much longer, due to its downgrading of essential services; sadly, another sign of the times.

I have planted trees that will be mature when my grandaughter's children are adults. They'll be able to say, "my great-gran planted this woodland". To have to end the project now, and dismantle everything I've built, would probably be the end for me. I don't know what else I can do. I'm 47. My mental health isn't brilliant. I no longer get every job I apply for like I did twenty years ago.

Back then, it was always assumed when I got older, I'd buy a farm or smallholding. My son's dad was a dairy farmer in Trelech. Their 200-acre farm had to be sold when his father and grandfather died, and all the relatives came out for their share. If OPD had existed then, the land could have been spilt and turned into separate holdings. Instead it was sold to a dog breeder.

Of course, the rise in house prices and the 2008 crash put paid to all of those ideas. But if I had been able to buy a farm, I'd still live according to OPD principles. The eco aspect of OPD should go without saying. All housing should have to have more ecologically sound rules imposed. What they call "traditional building" is going some way towards this but it's not enough and it's too slow.

Projects like OPD have the potential to solve the social housing crisis. Council purchased land, with modular homes, cheap to run and live in. The welfare bill is cut as there are no rents. There are no bills as the homes are off-grid. General well-being improves, then a side effect is less strain on the NHS. Happy people are less ill than distressed people, who currently often find themselves unable to secure themselves a home past their council flat tenancy, or uncertain, private short-let, unable to grow food because social housing is no longer like that of the fifties, where it was assumed people might like some outside space, where it was taken as said that people would grow their own provisions.

Now, with the popularity of the area as an ideal place for a second home, many locals have been completely priced out of the market. I have owned houses – I paid a mortgage alone for 16 years with two children. I missed a large part of their childhood because of this.

I have no inclination to exist in a consumerist world where one virus brings everything to a halt. Nature is showing us a very hard lesson right now. All I see on social media is people suddenly becoming interested in growing their own food. Change is coming. It took a virus, but something had to give eventually, and show the system for the unsustainable mess that it is. We all have to change every process in our lives. OPD is ready and waiting to be utilised to its maximum potential. It's a no-brainer.

It's been the worst experience of my life, far worse than divorce, a broken back, and losing my music shop! Waiting for planning, not knowing whether or not it was worth proceeding. It's been a very weird kind of limbo, and I really hope to be able to move on and continue what I've begun. I hope to able to replace my son's birthright in some small way. I myself have always felt rather rootless. All I'm really after is some solid roots, and a bit of room to grow.

17 THE LEVELLER

It's human nature to go into shock in an emergency, and it looks like the nation is in shock.

Here in Wales it has found its perfect manifestation. The public have again been split into opposite camps and the riots are about to begin.

As the schools closed and the sun came out, and Boris kept his advice just woozy enough to be indecipherable, the crowds flocked to Wales; here in West Wales Tenby, Saundersfoot and Newport were rammed with tourists. The second home owners had arrived, the camp sites filled up. In North Wales day trippers flocked to the Snowdonia National Park to out their hands all over the rocks. It seems similar scenes occurred in English seaside towns.

This has gone nuclear in this area. Facebook is awash with irate locals wondering why they have to lose their livelihoods, and close their bars, cafés and other public spaces, yet the tourists are turning up in their droves and licking their ice-creams as per tradition. We rely heavily on tourism in this area, but still, the people want the aliens to disperse. I've never seen such desperation.

If you're local, you're well aware that the local health services are stretched to breaking point at the best of times. The incomers don't realise this. They're used to just rocking up at A&E and filling out a form. In this county however, many people struggle to get a doctor's appointment in peacetime, let alone now. The wait in A &E is usually around 7 hours if you're lucky. All the shops are empty. Our infrastructure cannot cope with the incomers. We have thirty ventilators in Withybush hospital. It's a very big county. And that's our only hospital. And it's already broken past repair and essential services are being downgraded and shifted to Carmarthen, itself in need of a little TLC, to say the least.

Luckily, the big camp-site owners are closing down, the smaller will surely follow suit. One hopes that it's explained to people with houses in the county that refuse to go back to their primary address, that there are no beds in the hospital for them. And no food for them to buy.

And this is the interesting point. I see freedom loving people, myself included, desperately pleading for a lockdown. We don't want to take any chances with our elders, of which there are many in Pembrokeshire. If this is worse for the elderly then we're going to be inundated. 61% of the population of the county is over 60.

The trouble is with people not taking advice, is that it becomes necessary to impose and enforce rules. We become trapped in this purgatory of not wanting out liberties taken away, but not wanting our folks to die either. The shouting between the scared and the laissez faire is becoming as crass as the Brexit argument. That's the bit that hurts me the most in all of this. When we should come together, people are still finding ways to be at each others' throats.

My own hope is that the virus will turn out to be less lethal than we thought, and that we can get a hold on it. But one thing I would like to see, is a total break with the past in terms of the way we've been living. Some conspirators have suggested this is a hoax, or a drill. If it is, It has demonstrated that we're unready, to say the least.

If this is big, and real, then we should have been ready. It's not like we haven't known it's coming. It should have been a case of, oh well, here it is.. get the breathers out. Instead we're faced with this situation where the mighty are falling. Politically, physically, and economically.

The billionaires will escape this. They always do. The ones who I see getting affected the most are the middle classes. The working classes are used to this. Our lives fall apart most days. But to see the bourgeoisie getting upset at the lack of quinoa, and the loss of rent for their properties, and getting sent home from their holiday homes, and losing their assets with the fall in interest rates, and watching their unearned wealth disappear and the housing market inevitable drops to possibly and unprecedented, level, where the old money is suddenly worth a lot less than it used to be - it'll be interesting to see how it all pans out.

At the very least, the middle classes are experiencing the kind of insecurity and uncertainty that others face of a daily basis. Let's hope when this is all over, they remember what it feels like to be in crisis and to need assistance. We're always saying homelessness is two bad months away. Maybe we're about to level the land.

19 AN INSPECTOR CALLS

As my planning appeal hearing was cancelled due to Covid-19, I agreed with the planning inspectorate that I'd be happy to proceed through written representations, as I couldn't see the crisis ending anytime soon.

Pembs county council agreed, and more writing took place, the final comments as it were, having already had the final comments before the hearing. So, I made my final comments, others made their final comments. The Council made their final comments. Only one and a half pages, mostly just referring to the retrospective nature of my application. If only they knew the bungalow envy I suffer every time I drive through Efailwen and see the centrally heated homes all neatly lined up.

Anyhoo. After these final comments, I was told that I then had an opportunity to make final comments regarding the

Councils' final comments. So again, I made my final comments, mostly based around my bungalow envy., There have been so many final comments I'm running out of final comments, but the council always manage somehow to irritate me enough to make another final comment. So, I made my final comments.

Meanwhile, I was told the planning inspector would do a site visit, but as the council would not be present, I was not to approach him. I didn't move for a week. I watched, I analysed every dog bark, I peeped, but the guy is a ninja, because I didn't see him. However, I knew he'd been, because the process continued at the end of the week, thus demonstrated by the request for final comments on the final comments.

It's been three days since the final comments deadline. I've been told it can take up to six weeks for a decision to be made. I'm also aware that the planning inspectorate have been really quick dealing with every milestone of my case, so that makes me feel that I could get the decision any minute. So here I am, in lockdown, alone, in the place I'm not allowed to be, waiting for the word to say I can either be here or I can continue to not be.

The weirdness of life right now is surpassing every other time of life that I thought was weird. I should be climbing the walls by now. But I seem to have reached this state of Zen. Either that or delirium. Either way, ironically, for the first time ever, no one is coming to get me, because they're all on lockdown and working from home.

I've had a cough which didn't progress to anything but which has meant I have to stay put. It feels, for the first time, like I'm allowed to be here. I'm not sure whether to enjoy the feeling, or to not get too into it, just in case I get an email in a minute saying my appeal was refused. This is the most surreal limbo you can ever imagine, and I can't even go out for a bit to see a chum or the folks. How very ironic that is.

Half of me hopes that he takes ages to decide and leaves me be for a good few weeks with the illusion. The other half wants it over and done with, so I know whether or not I can relax or if I have to prepare for further battle.

On the plus side, the place is looking mega. I've planted extra veggies, instantly regretting it as I pot on a million cabbages, but I won't be regretting it when civilisation collapses. There are many people taking this opportunity to grow victory gardens, and I love that. I love that the crisis has made people see what's important. It certainly eliminates the bullshit. I usually wake up each day vaguely nervous that I've got to leave site and face the real world. At this moment, I can't, so all the guilt and stress of that thought is instantly dispersed. Knowing that you can't go anywhere is nice when you don't particularly want to go anywhere. All I have is this twilight time where I can reflect and observe the blossom on the fruit trees, the leaves and catkins busting from the willows, the veggies growing an inch a day in the polytunnel that I've finally got the way I want. There's new life everywhere, the bees are awake, the bird houses are filling up, the ground is drying and the air is full of singing birds, made louder by the lack of planes.

This feeling could last a day, or six weeks. If my appeal is successful it'll last forever. So, I'll just wait. And be happy for the present. Yes. That's what I'll do.

19 THE KING IS DEAD, LONG LIVE THE KING

There are battles, and then there are battles. Some are worth fighting, some are not.

Back when Blair took over the Labour party I wandered off, ignoring politics in my disillusionment, forming a liking for Charles Kennedy, even voting Lib Dems once.

When Corbyn rocked up, I couldn't believe it. I had it in my head that JC was the second coming. That he was going to bring Labour back to socialism, the way it was when I used to sit with my grandad and do the pools and watch the snooker.

I was born in the early seventies, so lived through a lot of crazy stuff as a child, the Falklands, the Miner's Strike, the troubles in Northern Ireland. Spitting Image was how my childish mind made sense of it all. I was incensed with

Thatcher over the school milk thing, and my grandad told me Tories were bad. When he had the opportunity to buy his council house for next to nothing he wouldn't, as he said social housing was for people that needed it. He lived in council houses for the rest of his life, downsizing as he went, before dying aged 92.

To me, because of his influence, socialism was a thing that just made sense and you never questioned it. It just was. The Labour party was an institution, like British Telecom, and Royal Mail, and British Rail and all the things that existed and were reassuring, and to be relied upon.

I didn't quite understand what was happening when it all got sold off. There was no logic to it. My brain didn't think in a capitalist way. The way the world became revealed to me made me disillusioned to the point that I felt I could no longer engage. So apart from turning up and dutifully voting Labour every time, even though they seemed to be creeping ever further away, Corbyn gave me the kind of impetus that makes you actually join a party, and join I did.

I watched closely as he became a hero, and I watched closely as he fell from grace. I grew frustrated with his silence over

Brexit, I became angry at his fence sitting, but I still wouldn't hear a word against him. I still won't. I met him, for a split second when he visited Haverfordwest in South West Wales - our local constituency county town - a few days before the election, and he gave me a hug. That positivity and elation stayed with me, right up to the moment that the exit poll was released.

I went to bed. And decided I'd had enough of politics. In the meantime, my pre-election spamming on Facebook had got so intense that I got reported and banned from posting for seven days.

Bored, and feeling like I had no voice, I wandered over to the old Twitter account I'd made ten years earlier, and starting floating around in there. I saw George Galloway had just started a new party. I watched the launch video and read the website. It said to be a member you had to get involved. I didn't want to. I was sick of shouting and not being heard. But as the weeks passed, and I started to calm down, I realised that the same was happening as when Corbyn appeared. There was something here that might be worth fighting for. I had a chat with George, and ten minutes later I had left Labour and joined The Worker's Party of Britain. It was that easy.

I met George when I went up to the rally in Brum. A nicer bloke you couldn't meet. Unassuming, no airs and graces, great hat. By the end of the day, and after all the talkers we had heard, I was more inspired than I had ever been by Labour. Everyone was on the same page. Everyone had a shared vision. The atmosphere in the room, filled with kids and friends and happy people, was one of family. And that feeling has continued. We have meetings online every week, a great side effect of the Coronovirus, in that we were forced to be creative about replacing the cancelled rallies. Hopefully this is something that will continue. Keeping in touch in this way ensures we all keep engaged, and we are encouraged to get involved.

There was never going to be a better opportunity for a socialist party, in that our capitalist government has been forced to turn to socialism to bail it out. The capitalist failures were exposed in less than a week, and the country doing the best out of everyone, really, is Cuba.

Socialism doesn't work, we keep getting told. That seems to me to be false, even more false now than ever. The Covid-19 crisis has changed things like never before, without warning. Capitalism has been dying a slow death; just hanging on, waiting for the end, a long, drawn out illness making it ever weaker. Covid has instead been the equivalent of a sudden accident, a car crash where capitalism finds itself with fatal injuries.

It surely can't recover, yet we know our corrupt governments will not rest until they've found a way to save its life, and they'll keep it on life support for as long as it needs to be, until it recovers. Someone has to be bold enough to sneak in and turn the plug off.

Who will that be? It's not going to be Labour. They're not holding anyone to account. The recent leaks throw up spectacular questions which we may or may not ever know the truth about. Labour isn't the King of the working classes any more. It hasn't been for a long, long time, since way before my grandad gave them credit for, but he was born in 1905, and was a product of his time.

Labour are making him turn in his British workman's grave. If he was alive today, I believe he'd join me in abandoning ship. You don't stay in a boat with a hole in it, not unless there's a good engineer on board. But let's be fair, a knight of the realm is never going to be much good with a spanner....

There's only one choice for socialism now, as far as I can see. Galloway has always stayed true to his word. What other politician has? Yes, he's changed his mind when presented with evidence, and that is the mark of a wise man. When people know what I've done, they say.. BIG BROTHER!!! Yes, he was on Big Brother, but if your only cultural reference of George is that, then I'm afraid you may be part of the problem my friend. Get on YouTube and watch his 43-minute speech where he rips the senate to shreds. Ten minutes in, you'll have forgotten all about that leotard.

Imagine if they'd told him to be a cat and he'd refused. What a pussy that would have made him. When you've got the bollocks to put that outfit on and raise a fortune for Palestinian kids, then I'll let you make fun. Until then, you're missing out bigly if you use something so trite to stop yourself from joining a party that is welcoming, true to its principles and its members. That is starting from the ground up and where your voice will be heard. Where you can learn so much from the amazing people that are on board. Joti Brar, deputy leader, is a legend in her own right, and the party is growing every day with people from all other parties, or with people that have finally found a party that works for them. It certainly works for me. And it couldn't have come at a better time.

Labour is gone. It's time to step up and be brave. To be the change and see the change.

The King is dead. Long live the King.

20 COMPUTER SAYS NO

The day before yesterday I got the email I had been dreading. I had again been refused. Not only that, but the enforcement order was to stay in place. I have nine months to take everything down, even the agricultural stuff like the polytunnel and goat house, the workshop and the caravan; everything must go, as the Manic Street Preachers once said. Something else they once said, those lovely Welsh boys is this. If you tolerate this, your children will be next. So, 36 hours after losing my entire future, I'm on track to making a few future decisions.

Firstly, I could go to the crown court. However, some friends of mine who won their case at crown court are now being taken back to court by the council who are appealing their crown court win. You couldn't make this stuff up.

Or, I could apply for agricultural business planning permission, and just not attempt to live here. After five winters in a field this is an attractive proposition. So, I spoke to the housing at the council. There are no council houses. The list is as long as my face was the day before yesterday. So, the Primary Mental Health Care Team put me in touch with another body that could apparently help with housing. Turns out, they basically act as an agent for people looking to rent. They don't have any secret houses available. Just the same ones that are on Zoopla. Which is none. There's a flat in Narberth, £129 a week. Their suggestion on paying that? Universal credit of course. To pay a private landlord a state subsidised rent that forces the tax payer to pay for a place for me to live even though I already have a place to live, the kind of place that the tax payer would really like to live too. What's wrong with this picture?

I could go full anarchy. I could just say, no, I'm not going. That's a possibility. In the spirit of Albert Dryden, I'd be into that while my strength held out. I could park my caravan in the council office car park. They have nice facilities. I could turn my place into a campsite, or gift it to the gypsies and move to Portugal. I could get lots of pigs.

In essence, I'm glad I didn't get OPD. It's not real freedom. The process has been the worst time of my life. Unimaginable stress and drip torture with all the waiting. It's flawed to the point of uselessness. There are so many loopholes that if your face doesn't fit or if you're retrospective in any way, you won't get it, simple as that. It's arbitrary and inconsistent. It's a policy that is not fit for purpose, when a holiday home owner can object to a local trying to live a sustainable life. If I live away from my land, I have to drive here every day. Logical that. In refusing OPDs they're forcing people back out into a system that doesn't work. Covid-19 has demonstrated how tenuous capitalism is. Yet, here I am, being told I have to go back out there into the machine.

I've been beaten by the system. A flawed, useless, not fit for purpose system. Against all logic, that is what has happened. So, we have no choice now but to change the system. And until then, I'm happy to ignore the system.

My entire future, home, business, the homes for my animals, everything, has all just been taken away from me. I now have nothing at all to lose. Nothing. I have no business to build any more, no home for my son to plan, no reason to care about any of it any more. The stress has gone. The wait is over. Now all I have is lots and lots of time, a blank canvass, nine months to decide what's next, and raise hell while I decide.

My objectors may have won this battle, but you know what they say about wars. And despite it all, I'm still happy. They have everything, yet they will never be happy. That's the difference between them and me. An I'd much rather be me.

21 THE BOOK OF REVELATION

I've been doing a bit of digging since my planning appeal was refused just over a week ago. Not garden digging. But digging into the planning history of the farm track where my land is, and where all my objectors have their properties.

I always knew that Anne Widdecombe's bunglow and the Katie Hopkins's holiday home had gone through on planning on the four- year rule, many years ago. It was a fact not lost on me when the owners started reporting me to the council repeatedly.

Widdeocmbe applied for retrospective planning on her block of four stables while my planning app was in. Mine took 18 months. Hers took 7 weeks. There were no drawings on her plans, and the community council said that the application was "vague", but it was passed by David Harries at PCC, nice and easy.

There was no talk of it being retrospective. And no talk of it being highly visible. The concrete floors, electricity, water, pretentious clock, were all deemed suitable to stay, even though she didn't ask permission first. What makes an application like that go through, and an application like mine to be refused?

Mr Bean in the farmhouse - a very well- respected architect, remember - who wrote a huge objection to my application, has a little cottage in his garden that he rents out. Turns out, this hasn't got planning permission. But it's been there long enough for the council to allow him to keep it. Funny that. He's got to apply for a certificate of lawfulness. Isn't that very suspicious? Someone who gets posh houses through planning as part of his job and has daily contact with the council would surely be very aware of the rules regarding planning. So it seems he was just trying to get away with it. And he has. They all have.

Hopkins and Noname like to tell the story of how they duped the planners by putting old soil between the stones so that when it was analysed it wasn't shown to be the concrete pointing that had actually been used.

Last year, Napolean cut my water pipes. During the ensuing arguments, Widdecombe told me he had planning permission for his buses and scrap yard, but it turns out that he doesn't. Yet no one on this track seems to mind his scrapyard, but they seem to take real umbridge to my cabbage patch.

The real point here, is the absolute two-facedness of a mafia ganging up on me when their noses are in no way clean, and they have ALL been in contravention or breach of planning. All of them. Yet the council saw fit to refuse the person who actually wants to farm this farmland, who actually asked for permission to build a house.

They have no need for the things they're allowed to keep. Hopkins and Noname have two cottages side by side in a village called Wilton in Wilshire, a village where the average house price is £700k. Two of them for Christ's sake. And yet another one here.

Napolean just inherited a cottage from an old lady up the road, so he has somewhere to live. Why is he still on the land, displaying a sold sign on the house, when the company whose sign he is using have never had the property on their books?

Why is Mr Bean allowed to rent out a second home without planning? Has he declared that income? Has he paid council tax? He's converted his sheds to a studio and a home for his flash sports car. But that's ok. Why?

The bunglow that was built on a wing and a prayer and got planning under four- year rule, but now also includes four stables outside the curtilage of the garden, is perfectly acceptable to the council. Why?

Point is, they got away with it because no one reported them. They've been sneaking about down this track for years. Yet as soon as someone else does something they're straight on the complain and object train. Surely that's the worst kind of hypocrisy? To be so blind to your own activities while judging and slandering someone else? To insist no one else has an opportunity, even though you've all been doing exactly whatever the hell you want? I don't think so.

I don't suppose they ever expected their stories to see the light of day. When they began their campaign of bullying I was in the middle of a divorce, weak, exhausted and alone. That's not the case anymore. I'm going to fight this to the death. Mark my words. They have holiday homes, rental properties, stables, spare cottages. All I want is a home.

22 And Justice For All . . . ?

I found a house available to rent. I looked at my finances. Not a hope. So I looked into Universal Credit, like the council advised me to when they told me I have to leave my super cheap eco residence that I build out of swamp and that costs nothing to live in.

Guess what? Because I'm self-employed, and I own a bit of ex swamp, then the amount of UI I'd be able to claim wouldn't be enough to keep me in teabags, let alone rent a house and pay all the bills.

So of course, this leaves me where exactly? The council are dying to classify me as homeless. I'm not sure why, because with that status the only place on offer to live is in the hostel in Pembroke, about 50 minutes' drive from the livestock. It's a bit rich refusing me OPD because I'm not considered eco enough and then attempting to force me to drive 60 miles a day to my place of work.

The lady who put me on the council housing list actually said to me, and I quote, "It sounds like you have a smallholding there. Is a council house really right for you?" This was of course after telling me that I'd never get one. Because there aren't any. And I know there aren't any. I've lived in a field for five years. I'm fully aware of the lack of affordable housing.

My reaction to all of this has been to move my caravan. Not off my plot. But further onto it. Onto a bit that you couldn't drive onto in October when I brought the caravan here. I'm now next to the dried-up pond, down in the space where I was planning to build my house. It's like being on holiday. I'm legit able to stay here until February, so I may as well have a good time.

Last week I took the plunge and made an official complaint to Mr Bean's architectural firm. I was shaking as I wrote it. It's not in my nature to write Karen-esque letters to complain. The response came quickly, and was basically a very long rambling excuse for not having planning permission on his cottage, by telling me all about how I should have applied for planning permission before I spent any time and energy on my project. Then he asked if I have any herbs for sale. I'm not making this up, honest. Sorry we made you homeless, but are you still planning to sell cheap plants? In answer, yes, I am still selling cheap plants. Just not here. I'm selling them in South Pembs where the neighbours appreciate it. I would be selling cheap plants right next door to you, had I got Planning. However, that's a decision that you took. Garden Centre next door or not? Hmm. I've decided not. Well, there we are then. You don't get no herbs.

He also told me that it's a myth that there is corruption in the council regarding planning. It's not a myth. The myth that it's a myth is spread around by the people who don't want the layman to know what really goes on, because they think we're stupid and that people don't talk.

I'm not sure if RIBA will do anything about his transgressions. He said that the other things I've mentioned, i.e. landlord registration, septic tank issues, Energy Performance Certificate, have either been "sorted" or will be after Covid. No details. I can assume from the way he fights about his right to keep his cottage and not need a Certificate of Lawfulness, that he would fight to defend himself in all matters. I can only surmise, then, that he isn't registered as a landlord, and hasn't registered the dodgy septic tank, and doesn't have an energy performance certificate, among other things. Prove me wrong.

It feels weird to get all Karen, and do the reporting thing. But needs must, when the devil vomits in your kettle, as they say. I'm not really prepared to sit back and let this injustice go. The only reason the neighbours here got away with all their planning transgressions, is because no-one grassed them up. I still haven't had a satisfactory answer from the council about how they came to the decision to grant retrospective planning on Widdecombe's stables. And I won't get an answer. In the same way that they just shrug when I ask if they're going to enforce the rental property next door. They're not going to, of course. They only enforce people they think they can get away with enforcing.

Mr Bean's letter also contained a warning to take down my structures before the deadline. Not a trace of irony. To quote Blackadder again. Irony. It's like goldy and bronzy, only it's made of iron.

Like my resolve, Mush.

29 CHARGE!

In a recent post on the one planet council Facebook page, David Thorpe stated that some OPDs get support from the One Planet Council, that is, if they are considered worthy. I have only seen one letter of support for an OPD from the OPC and that was one whereby the couple involved attended one of David's courses on how to do OPD.

These courses go through the practical ins-and-outs of the paperwork, they brush stroke over permaculture principles, they talk about eco building, but I feel that there should be a course that describes the painful process that OPD is. Perhaps this book is that course! David has a book out about OPD which is forty quid to buy. This is £8.99 – possibly even cheaper if you can pick up one of the second hand copies that my neighbours will be selling once they've read it to see if they're in it.

The problem with only supporting OPDs that the OPC deem worthy, is a bit like them saying, we feel that these other applications are shit. Don't pass them, council. If the OPC is there to support, then they should support everyone, and if they see someone in need of help, they should help. I know it's run by volunteers, but in order to encourage OPD, they're going to have to come up with ways of helping people get things passed, otherwise, the OPC become as redundant as OPD itself. Either that, or have a blanket policy of not endorsing any at all. But then, that sort of seems pointless too.

The OPC page is a bit of a telephone directory for OPD services. Apart of course from Pete Linnell who spends hours helping people, above and beyond the call of duty. He's done more for OPD that anyone. He sees it for what it could be, not just for what it is. And every time I give the policy a hard time, I feel bad, like I'm being mean to Pete, because he fights so hard for it all the bloody time. If it wasn't for the respect I have for that old bugger, I wouldn't be watching my tongue at all.

OPD is not easily achievable, no matter what your course tells you, although if you put enough coins in the machine you will get it eventually. These courses tell you that, but they don't really mention the coins in the machine bit. OPD is sold as the holy grail, the ticket to a country life, painted as perfect and pure. But there are some established OPDs that are struggling with the workload, having realised what a sketch it is to be relying on a cabbage patch sans slug pellets. It's not all flowy dresses and berries. Much discussion has been taking place this week around how much to charge people to visit your OPD. To me, this seems crazy. As part of OPD you're supposed to give something back to the community, via open days and suchlike. That's a captive audience and free rein to set up shop. A brilliant opportunity to sell your produce and network and advertise. That's community sharing, isn't it? Charging for entry turns OPD into exclusive curios. The argument is that it's time consuming to talk to people and it stops you doing your work. If people are interested, when they come round, get them involved in the work. You say they're coming to learn, well, then teach them something. Then they'll probably buy some plants off you and a puppet if you've got some. Is that really not enough? Is it all about profit and ticket prices? Little petting zoos all over the place where you get to pet the hippies? Yes, you'll have wisdom to share, but I don't remember our ancestors charging a couple of bob before they passed on the verbal knowledge of what plants are safe to eat.

If people want to donate to your project during their visit, then they will, and that's fine. That's up to them. If you do your job and talk them into doing OPD, which is surely the point, then your reward can be that you have helped make it easier for those coming after you. No? The fact that it's not seems to tap at the drum of what I feel is wrong with OPD in its present form. It's not inclusive enough. It's becoming an exclusive club of exemplars, all feeling like they won the game.

But is it really about being exemplar? Who gets to say Cornerwood aren't exemplar? I've been seeing posts for months, while we had that drought, that all the trees are dying on the OPDs. Mine aren't. Mine survived really well because of the high-water table that everyone insisted meant that I couldn't grow trees.

If I wanted to, I could keep fighting, but it would cost, emotionally and monetarily. It's all just a very expensive dance. If you run out of coins then it's game over, just like down Tenby arcade.

If you've got a pitless bottom, well, then you're laughing. You'll get OPD. Eventually. It won't matter how long it takes either, because you'll probably be ok in your rented house until you succeed. Renting a house is only an issue if you can't sustain a house, land, a job, a management plan and all the other stuff that getting OPD entails. My point is, it's not the answer to social housing, like I hoped it would be. It's not even close. It's also so exclusive with so few people doing it that it can't really be said to be improving the carbon footprint of Wales. In fact, most people who have OPD moved to Wales to get it, so one could argue that Wales's carbon footprint has actually gone up a bit.

Not to mention all those pieces of paper, and manhours, and resources that are spent on each application. It probably cost PCC around 20k to take me to appeal. It'll cost them another bunch of cash to bulldoze me if that's the way things eventually go. Then they'll have to help house me. How are they gonna do that exactly? We've already seen that they can't.

OPD is far too long winded and exclusive to be of any use in the current housing or ecological crisis. It's too small. And while it remains the way it is, it will stay small.

Approved OPDs want you to sell it, to big it up, to encourage others to do it. I was talked into it, when the advice really should have been, don't bother, you're gonna have to give up before you win because it's all about resources.

I should have applied for seasonal worker instead, or rural enterprise development, but there we are. Hindsight is indeed a wonderful thing. But it's like childbirth. No one told me how much that hurt before I did it, and therefore the surprise of all that pain nearly killed me more than the pain did. I'm not gonna sit here and tell you this shit doesn't hurt. It really does. And in certain cases, could probably destroy you. There are stories of relationship breakups, lost land, lost money, lost sanity... all sorts of lives have been changed for the worse by their encounter with this policy. The policy needs rewriting if it's to continue, and fast. Or it'll burn out very quickly. It's gone on as long as it has because people have believed in it. I did. I don't anymore. It's a flawed and inconsistent system, full of loopholes which the councils have discovered and can use to stop you if your face doesn't fit.

If someone asked me, should I try OPD, I'd say, if you have the budget for three years rent, and the dosh to pay someone to do it, or the kind of academic mind that can do it yourself, and you're ok with waiting, and monitoring reports, etc, then you could give it a go. You'll get it eventually. Chances are, if you're that kind of person, then it's quite probably within your means to buy a little smallholding, especially if you're selling property in England. If that's the case. You'd be nuts to do OPD. You can live off grid in a ready-made house you know. You don't have to go batty over it.

Many people have more than twelve acres and they do OPD. This also confuses me, when you have so many more ways to live on land if it's more than twelve acres. Don't ask me about that stuff. Ask Pete Linnell. And if you ask him and you win the game, get him a bottle of scotch.

24 THE SHOW MUST GO ON

My plan, when I began documenting this journey, was never to be the harbinger of doom for the OPD movement. I was always sticking up for OPD on the fb page, telling people that said it was impossible without loads of cash, that it WAS possible and that I was living proof. I'd bought marginal land, at a bargain price. I'd improved it and made it work. I had been told before applying that it was a policy that was watertight. That if you ticked all the boxes then they had to grant you permission. And if they didn't, then you would win at appeal, because everyone wins at appeal.

These things are clearly not true and I found out the hard way. I'm not going to sit by and watch other people be drawn in and fooled in the same way.

My friend sold his profitable business to do OPD. He has land and is half way through the process of applying. He was optimistic, like I was. He'd been told what I was told.

Now he's crapping himself. We met on the OPD FB page, five years ago, green as hell, both asking stupid questions. The answers you got back then were very different to the answers you get to the same questions now. What happened to every piece of land in Wales has outline planning for OPD?

I got to the chase first and he's watched me go through hell. Now he's following behind me with his own project. But he's no longer confident. He's seen the whole bloody process from start to finish and beyond. He's understandably worried.

I know that I'm not in the good books of the OPC. I don't blame them for that. They're trying really hard to fight the good fight for a movement that began with such promise, but unfortunately, with the loss of support in Parliament, and the lack of individuals in power who support the scheme, and the arbitrary way in which LPAs can make things up as they go along, and differ so widely in attitudes that Caerphilly Council are encouraging OPD and others are clearly not, it seems that a losing battle is being fought and that OPD is now just another Place in the Country type fad.

I've been told to not diss the policy, as the policy is not at fault. But a policy should be able to be applied by a multitude of protagonists with uniform results. That's what a policy is. However, that is clearly not the case in this instance. A policy can only be as good as those who are in charge of its operation. If it's not going to be applied consistently, then I'd go as far as to say that it's not a policy. It's just plain old discretionary planning permission.

OPD was, I thought, supposed to answer a legitimate, community housing need. People choosing to live a low impact alternative lifestyle. There's nothing alternative about OPD as it exists now. If you have the means, you can buy the best land, hire the best people to write your plan, hire the best lawyers, and hey presto.. planning permission. Same as it ever was. Many people who currently have OPD permission are not living on their site. They're living in accommodation elsewhere and building their dream home from afar. That's self-build. To me, OPD is creating your space around you, as simply as your needs allow – isn't it?

There's a roundhouse with 80 acres of woodland that's just come on the market. It's half a million quid. The agents haven't taken photos of the woodland. Just the hobbit house. That, ladies and gents, is called "agents knowing their market".

I'm not dissing OPD, or the people who have been successful. But to expect me to not react with some bitterness and anger would be to assume that I'm Hercules. I'm not. I'm not a hippy living in fairyland either. I'm just a local kid who made tons of mistakes and will never be permitted to forget them. Apparently if I'd had a community meeting none of this would have happened. At least that's what David Thorpe and others on the Facebook OPC page told me. Yet the approved OPDs locally did not have community meetings. They also tried to say that I failed because I was retrospective, yet a retrospective application was approved just a couple of weeks after mine was refused.

The official line given by the planning inspectorate was that my application wasn't written by a competent person, even though it was prepared by Tao, who had done lots of successful OPDs. They didn't know that he had written it. They assumed it was me, revealing that their decision was prejudiced, and not based on the information presented to them, but on an assumption about my personal capabilities. The refusal also implied that a single woman couldn't possibly achieve the aims stated on the management plan. In fact, not one single woman OPD has been passed first time out. Of the three that have tried, including myself, one got hers at appeal, another, a lovely lady I spoke to called Sue Galooly, was refused twice at appeal. She's still fighting, and I'm behind her all the way. Single men have applied and been successful.

The people judging me on my wrongs, only know the bits, or care about the bits, where I messed up. When I'm right, no-one remembers, when I'm wrong, no-one forgets.

There are people on the OPC page who are, and never will be, anything to do with OPD. They're there for what reason? I see them like the posts where my failures are highlighted. They're people who used to be on my friends list on FB, but made judgements and then deleted me. Now they like nothing more than to watch me suffer. But that's ok. Their weird little lives are empty, and that's no concern of mine. On the other hand, I've had so many messages of support I'm touched beyond words, which is not like me at all! I've had lovely words, offers of places to stay, made new friends, re-engaged with old ones. I'd like to thank those people. They know who they are.

People are treating me with kindness and humility and humanity and compassion and understanding, leaving aside judgement, because they know what it's like to be in the positions I've been in, because they've actually taken notice of the Tess behind the online, angry persona Tess, that the others all like to think they know.

To the friends old and new, who get it, and have been there for me, and who stick their necks out, and who show solidarity, I thank you and I love you. You're all mega.

Finally, with all that's going on globally, how can any of this even be an issue? Who cares? As usual the main point of someone just needing a home is completely missed. My tiny life is a microcosm of that insane, macro world out there. All the madness, all the fighting, all the wars... it exists here in miniature. What a load of nonsense it all is. I have no control of any of out there, but I have control of in here. I'm entitled to tell my story. To fight the small battles in my little world. And to give people the warning and flip side in order to make informed decisions.

And so I continue with the show. It's all I really know how to do innit,. theatre. Apart from making a lovely cup of tea....

25 EVERY CLOUD

They say that all good things must come to an end. My affair with OPD is well and truly over. That ship has sailed. It's had its chips. It's good night Vienna. It's good night from me, and it's good night from him. Good night, and God bless.

But they also say, when one door opens, another closes, or is it the other way around? Sometimes you're in a revolving door, and you can't get out, or there's a revolving door, and you can't get in to use the door.

It's been a couple of months now since my refusal, and I'm starting to be able to view it objectively. I had no idea how much it was stressing me out, but now I'm on the outside I can see really clearly that the whole process was the main cause of all my life's stress. I went to Tesco's yesterday. Twice. Two different Tesco's. Why is this news? Well, because a year ago that would have been impossible. One

Tesco would have been impossible. Most days I could barely make it to the village. My anxiety levels were like nothing I've ever experienced, and coming on the back of divorce and all that, it was too much. Every failed cabbage was a crisis terror. Every moment I felt I was being watched by neighbours. Every moment I was being assessed and photographed and spied on. Every journey I made, every Facebook post, everything I did was under scrutiny. Every dog bark made me jump in fear. Every car on the track filled me with adrenaline. Every moment of every day was dictated to by the nervy feeling of uncertainty. Every sentence began with "…if I get my planning", every plan had to wait, every idea had to analysed for suitability, everything had to be planned. All spontaneity was gone. My life was one long cyclorama of vivid dreams, suspicion and dread. I'm not really sure how I got through it. Although I have a clue.

I was watching an episode of Renegade Inc. the other day with Dan. It was talking about the fall of empires, and I couldn't help feeling like they were talking about OPD. Its rise, its success, its apparent authority, and then the potential for the destruction of its own self. There's a lot of interest in OPD at the moment. It's becoming big business. Maybe it's at its zenith, or maybe it's still on the rise. Maybe it's already had its day. Time will tell.

Anyway. Dan. You remember him. The Dan who got OPD. Our tree surgeon buddy. What happened to him? I hear you ask. Well, as we speak, I'm sitting at the table outside his caravan on his OPD in Reynalton, writing this while he chats to his brother. We've been making a path with timber and woodchip. It looks ace.

I obviously met Dan through doing OPD. We were both putting our management plans together at the same time. I knew him loosely from 20 or so years ago. He used to go out with my friend Emma and they had a kid, Will.

Will is now 18 and is a tree surgeon himself. I tease him about changing his nappy. Me and Dan ended up bonding over our hate for the council and our vitriol over the long wait. The 18 months we spent waiting for a decision ended at the same time, although it took the council all that time to make one decision on his case, and I managed to fit two refusals, an appeal and an enforcement into the same timescale.

And now I find myself with a nice boyfriend, who has helped me through all the agro, and kept me sane through the process. The stress we were both under could have gone two ways. Once the planning decision had been made, we could have easily drifted apart, our time together over, both on separate missions. But as it turns out, he has OPD, and I don't. And the irony is, we'd like to move in together, but for me to move to his place would mean that he has to adjust his entire management plan to accommodate an extra personage. It would be even harder to take Albee. And that's not something I'm prepared to put him through. We're well aware of what the council are like, and we're well aware of what a delight the council think I am. I'm pretty sure Dan's OPD decision took such a long time because of his association with me. Luckily, him being a respected local businessman who knows everyone, including members of his community council, meant that much as the planning officers tried to refuse him, they couldn't. They looked everywhere for that little gap to say no, and they couldn't find one. He wasn't retrospective, he didn't move onto his land, his management plan was perfect, he already had financial proof of his ability to make money through wood carvings, and there it was. Scuppered, council. Too bad. But I bet you a crisp pound note if I set any kind of foot on the place, they'll take it all away from him. At least, that's my fear.

Even so, our paths are not going to split. They're staying very firmly together. As an OPD you're allowed to have volunteers, and so I can go and park at his place sometimes and help plant his gardens and build paths and make fences and do all the stuff I was going to do here, but do it there instead. He's helped me make my place look good with the raised beds and the woodchip built from tree surgery waste that he brought to mine, and so we've had a really good practice, and done lots of experimenting, ready to make his place fabulous. If I do want to sell, which is a possibility, and I've had offers, then, someone will be getting a really nice, organized and productive plot.

As far as where do I live? Well, I don't know. What's live? Sleep? I can work at my land every day if I want, and go somewhere else to sleep every night and that doesn't constitute living. Does it? What does? Home is where the heart is, isn't it?

Mine is scattered, and has been for ages. The mission has to be to sort out a house for me and Alb, now that it seems to be pretty easy to get a mortgage all of a sudden, and now that the housing market is crashing, and property prices are coming down. Capitalism has done its thing. The wheel turns, and every now and again the door opens to get back onto the ladder. It'll be a while before I can get that elusive farm, but that's always going to be the plan. Space for everyone to be together. The horses are on rented land again. The goats and pets are at Wern. Dan is here at Reynalton. Kino is in the Dock. Albee is mostly in Llandissilio. My folks are in Jameston and Frome, my granddaughter Lilly is in Milford, my brother in Cornwall.... They're my heart, and I'm separated from all of them. Or perhaps I share myself between them. I guess until I find sold ground that's what I'll do.

But for now, the most solid ground I've ever had is Dan. Without him I would never have survived this process. Like, proper seriously. When the neighbours conned me into going to a meeting about the track, an obvious ambush, Dan came with me. Stern words were starting to be spoken over the table, and all I could feel was Dan kicking my leg under it. I was just about to turn and snap at him and say, "stop kicking me I'm trying to shout at this woman!" But then realised that's why he was kicking me, so that I didn't. So that I kept my cool. That's what they wanted, and he stopped it.

He also came with me to fix the water pipes when they got cut. He was there when Widdecombe called me mental and told me no-one liked me. He was there when she told me off for picking up one of her stones and forbidding me to use it to weigh down the water pipe in its new place after the fix. He saw it all. He heard it all. He protected me from it all. And ultimately, the best thing to come out of all of this is him.

They thought they made me homeless. But they were wrong. Dan was home all along.

I am home.

EPILOGUE

Don't cry. It's not that bad. In fact, I'm happier right now that I've been for ages. I've got regular writing work, and I've formally announced my candidacy against Huw George for the next county elections. I don't even need Prozac anymore. It's all good, man.

I still believe that OPD has potential, but not as it is. I believe that councils should be seriously looking at this. They need to provide social housing somehow, and this could be a really quick, cheap and sustainable way of doing it. Of course, to get any ideas like this into the open, you really need to be putting your head above the parapet. What, even more? Yep. Even more. You need to get into politics.

I'm pretty sure Huw George has heard by now that I intend to run against him. He's been there for twelve years. Budge up Huw, let the young 'uns have a go! He may be regretting not helping me out. Let's face it, he could have kept me contained in a field with my cabbages, quiet and well behaved. Yet instead he chose to awake the devil in me. Ah well. Tough call, Huw.

I find the amount of drama associated with this application incredible. At the end of the day, it's just a planning application. How the hell do you manage to get a book out of a planning application? Talk about do me a favour.

And if I hadn't been refused the first time, I wouldn't have written my first bit for the Herald, and then wouldn't have got a column in the Herald, and so I wouldn't have got the articles into the Morning Star, and they wouldn't have been spotted by The Land Magazine. You see how it works?

If I hadn't been so pissed off with the Labour party at exactly the same time as I was getting let down by my local councillor, I would never have contacted George Galloway, and we would never have had that phone conversation where he persuaded me that to run for MP would be really good fun. If I still feel like it when the elections come round, I'll be putting myself up for the Worker's Party candidacy in North Pembs. All good news for my other OPD nemesis, Stephen Crabb.

And the most fun news of all, is that my neighbours got wind of the fact that I might be selling my land. Now they want to make an offer. Would you Adam and Eve it? They're obviously aware that I sold Darklands to three generations of motorcycle and quad racers. Yes I did. And I'd do it again. My neighbours must be more than a little bit worried about whose hands this place may end up in. I would be, if I was them. But you know, neighbours - and I know you're reading this - everything's for sale. For a price. Bear in mind that the agents are currently out valuing hobbit houses for half a million quid, not to mention that 2.79 acre plot in St David's for 35k. My God, you may even awake the capitalist in me. Cynical? I'm getting there, yeh.

So you see, it never really pays to pick on someone who you think is weak, and who you think has no way of ever defending themselves. You should always remember, before deciding to be a big bully, that you never really know who you're dealing with. Especially if you're not local.

Ha.

Appendices – Pete Linnell

Appendix 1 – Process

Narratives of obstruction.

An exploration of how antagonistic narratives can result in delay and constraint on roll out of Welsh government OPD policy objectives. This being a case study of the process of an OPD application for land at Wern Isaf, Pembrokeshire. Ref 19/0190/PA

Abstract

TAN6/ OPD is being cited as contrary to Local Plan policies in parts of Wales, including in the officers' report for this case. The narrative impact of this, and how this determines the delegated decision pathway are explored in the light of this case. The support for the policy from the Planning Inspectorate is recognised and welcomed, providing LPAs with clear messages about how they are to treat OPD applications as distinct from conventional forms of land use and housing. Suggestions are made for LPAs to adopt supplementary policies at once to show support for OPD in recognition of the part it plays in mitigating Climate Emergency.

The specific case study here examines the policies and procedures of Pembrokeshire planning department. References are made in passing to other LPAs to offer contrasts, but other LPA process and policies have not yet been examined in detail. There is merit in examining such for all Welsh LPAs to ensure continuing roll out of OPD across the whole of Wales, time and resource constraints presently prevent this.

Pembrokeshire is very much at the heart of Welsh One Planet Development, it is where the challenging projects at Brithdir Mawr (www.thatroundhouse.info) gave rise to the pressure for policy change at local level, and subsequently home to the Lammas eco-village- the largest project of its kind in the UK and whose struggle for planning consent within policy 52 led directly to creation of TAN6/ OPD at national level. (www.lammas.org.uk) Today, Pembrokeshire has the largest number of OPD plots in addition to those consented under the local LID Policy

(Policy 52). It is worth noting that Pembrokeshire County Council has declared a Climate Emergency.

It would be easy to assume therefore that this county is open and welcoming to OPD pioneers, and that they would be confident to be given consent for any well-prepared application. It would also be reasonable to expect that both planners and elected councillors (especially Planning Committee members) would by now be thoroughly attuned to both the letter and spirit of the national policy and its guidance documents.

Despite this, within the last year, there have been public comments about OPD which reveal both a lack of understanding of the requirements and practices of the policy and hostility to the objectives of the national policy. In addition, there has been a singular failure to connect the Council's (indeed the nation's) declaration of Climate Emergency with deployment of the only immediate practical solution available to those who are ready and willing to live a testably sustainable life.

Elected councillors are of course at liberty to hold any views they wish, but when considering the local application of national legislation, they have a clear duty to remain impartial and to apply their powers according to the rule of law; failure to do so results in costly appeals or even legal action. The duty of impartiality is even more clear in the case of planning officers, as public servants trained in planning law and practice they are expected to examine applications put to them and make decisions under delegated powers or recommendations for decisions at committee. What follows reveals how a counter narrative is impacting the further deployment of OPD in practice in this county.

PCC planning department uses its own locally determined decision rule for the processing of applications under delegated powers. Whilst this is true of all LPAs, the PCC version is subtly at variance with that of the neighbours in Carmarthenshire- and most other LPAs with which this writer has had dealings. (Table1)

All applications are examined by officers, working as individuals or in teams for larger more complex cases; these officers will report to their senior officer who will make the decision to determine the application herself or pass it to a committee (of elected members) for determination. The rule by which this choice is made is of interest here.

I quote from an email sent by the PCC case officer to the applicant

"Applications which are typically presented to planning committee are larger scale developments or those which are recommended for approval contrary to the Local Development Plan (LDP). Therefore the number of objections received does not influence the method of determination. Due to the current policies in the LDP, the only OPD applications which are presented to planning committee are those which are recommended for approval by officers.

Table 1. Delegated decision option matrix

Table 1. Delegated decision option matrix		
	Officer recommendation	
	Approve	Refuse
Application consistent with LP policies	Approval	?

| Application not consistent | To Committee | Delegated refusal |

Appendix 2 - Reflections on the outcome of the appeal for OPD at Wern Isaf – Pete Linnell

At first blush I was shocked. Despite all my years of dealing with contested planning issues I retain the capacity to be shocked by a decision- and the manner in which it was delivered. The decision looks at first to be capricious, random, unreasonable and brutal in its impacts on the life of the applicant and her family. So much so that I am minded of the analyst's appraisal of US foreign policy under Bush Junior- if you lash out at random your foes will never be able to predict, and thus plan around, your actions. It behoves us that care about these things to subject this decision to some deeper analysis in an attempt to find in it the lessons we can take forward, and how it can inform the advice and guidance we are able to offer future aspirants to Welsh TAN6 One Planet life2. We need to be clear about the facts of the case, and we also need to deploy some recognised theory-based tools to unpack meaning from the facts. The range of tools which could be used is surprisingly broad.

Let us begin with an examination of what constitutes facts in this case. It begins with the obvious observation, which I am confident will not be disputed, that Ms. D has undertaken operational development on her land, which land does not enjoy permitted development rights due to the holding being below the threshold area. The nature and meaning of the various structures and activities on the land however are not so straightforward as may first appear- to Ms. D each element has its place in the pattern of her land use and animal husbandry efforts but to the objectors to her plan all they see is a jumble of random repurposed assemblages- vehicle bodies, sheds and caravans. The introduction of these elements onto the land is an action that normally requires formal planning permission (in the absence of PD rights) so as a responsible citizen Ms. D applied under the most appropriate policy option available to her- the TAN6 OPD policy of the Welsh Government.

The application generated considerable documentation, which remains available for scrutiny on the Pembs. County Council (PCC) website3. The first application was refused and followed by a resubmission which addressed the reasons for refusal given for the original. An independent expert helped prepare the second application and declared it robust in response to the original rejection. It was the refusal of this application which led to the appeal. In addition, as soon as the second application was refused PCC served an enforcement notice on Ms. D. which also was simultaneously appealed.

In addition to the publicly shared documents Ms. D. also made an FOI request of PCC for all material pertaining to her application and discovered that the planning officer had been encouraging her neighbours, (who objected to the application) to photograph and report on any activity on the land. This raises questions about other relevant facts which are concealed by virtue of not being part of the written record, nor available to the FOI request. Examples would be verbal interactions between officers within the hierarchy of the office, between members of the public and officers or elected members. We have no way of discovering the existence, timing or content of any such interactions- even in a court of law under oath a witness can suffer amnesia of detail.

As part of the appeal process the inspector made a site visit, and commented on his observations in his report. Ms. D reports that she was never informed of the time of his visit and was never given the opportunity to agree a safe protocol for the inspector to properly examine her project and question her about any aspect of her work. She has no proof that the visit actually took place.

In the normal course of such cases the appeal would have been dealt with by way of a full public enquiry- allowing all the stakeholders to present their evidence and respond to questions in an open and public way- all on the record of sound and video recordings. It remains the case however that despite the very public taking of evidence, such an inquiry may often be little more than a De Bordian spectacle4- with the decision ultimately made on the inspector's own reading of the evidence. In this case we were denied the public examination- all we have left is the script- being the written and drawn documents presented as the application itself, the responses from consultees both statutory and public, the officer's report and final summary documents submitted by both "sides". And of course, the decision letter.

There remain many other levels of facts pertinent to this case; from the development actions of neighbours, through local socio-economic and political realities to the original objectives of the Welsh Government in creating TAN6 OPD policy at the outset. Obviously, none of these were considered by the inspector, but he does admit to being guided by the same government guidance notes which inform applicants and officers on the practical application of the policy. Also pertinent is the locally decided delegated decision matrix by which PCC planners decide which applications go before elected members. A document I prepared examining this aspect of this case was dismissed by the inspector despite the crucial role the decision matrix played in the refusal of the application.

At this point we can consider an analysis of the script from a legal context. As resort to legal action is the only remaining option for Ms. D. to carry her case further she would need to take appropriate advice (I am not a lawyer) but it seems to me that the process of determining her application has been riddled with errors of omission and commission which would render it vulnerable to legal challenge if Ms. D. were possessed of the means to sustain an action through the courts.

Here we have lesson one from this decision. Legal remedy is only available to those with spare resources which can be put at risk by court action. Consequently, those with limited means do not have access to all the options available to secure an OPD consent in the face of determined local opposition.

In light of the decision, and her perception of having been let down by her local councillor (who has previously expressed opposition to OPD and asked for a moratorium on new OPD applications. In this case he offered to help the applicant but in reality, failed to bring the case to the elected planning committee.) the applicant is taking a highly Habermassian civil society5 line by declaring her intention to contest the local council seat at the next election. The Party under whose flag she will do this has a very clear understanding of the meaning of what has happened to her. By attempting to take control of one of the key means of production, productive land, she has challenged the hegemony of the owner class; to whose benefit the entire fabric of the rule of law- and specifically the right to control how land is used- has been produced for the last few hundred years. It comes as no surprise to them that she has been refused consent to meet her own needs directly from her own land- and so not have to pay rent or sell her labour power; free from exploitation by the owner class.6

In the script of TAN6 OPD is emphasised that the dwelling on land allowed under this policy is exceptional. This is writ large in the original note and reinforced strongly in the subsequent guidance notes7- repeating the framing of OPD as an exception to "normal" policies against new dwellings in the "countryside". Along with this exceptionalism then is extra baggage of justification- for an application to succeed it must pass a series of demanding tests- failure, even partial, on any one of these has been used as grounds for refusal. This exceptionalism also then permits LPAs to frame OPD- a Welsh Government policy- as being contrary to local policies which "normally" do not permit new dwellings in the countryside. This framing thus creates at the outset a narrative of opposition, of being contrary to locally decided policies. This will sit well with the political stance of those councils who are dominated by parties which do not have power in the Welsh Parliament, providing an opportunity to exercise power locally over matters the Government is attempting to change for the benefit of the nation.

Normalisation of the idea that new dwellings in the countryside are bad also suits the agendas of the status quo. This idea is heavily freighted with the values of the "picturesque landscape" school of aesthetics prevalent around the turn of the 20th century and later embodied into the founding principles of organisations such as the Council for the Protection of Rural England (same scripts apply to Wales). The specific trigger for this organisation was the emergence of plotland settlements following WW1 and this narrative- to keep working class people from having ownership of even small plots of land in rural areas is the foundational narrative of the policies still prevalent today. From Ward[8] to Fairlie[9] theorists and practitioners of a return to the land movement have recognised that their objectives would bring them into conflict with the power of the wealthy owners of the land- by challenging their "god given" right to exploit and enjoy the land and all its creatures for their own absolute enjoyment.10 In the light of Climate Emergency, those who would address how to meet their own needs without imposing a burden on either other people today or everyone in the future are being restrained by the power of obsolete paradigms of control over both land and the decisions about what can be done on it and by whom. In Foucauldian5 terms the entire basis of the UK development control apparatus is about the use of established power to maintain itself and the status quo. If the "Landscape" is a text, "The Countryside" is a radical conservative polemic.

Lesson three from this decision tells us that the powerful have everything set up the way they want, and if you try to encroach upon their enjoyment the existing power structures are configured to serve their interests- not yours. This is evidenced by the immediate deployment of enforcement notification following the second refusal emphasising the location of the applicant as being in conflict with the established local order.

Returning to this work after some days have passed; the original break caused by my own lack of experience and training in the body of work and knowledge I am about to bring into this analysis- namely Feminist Critical Theory. As this piece is not intended as a fully referenced academic work but more of a scoping polemic, I beg forgiveness for making general points with no supporting citations.

There is a thread running through the inspector's report which spins up to weave the final conclusion and lay its smothering blanket over Ms. D's aspiration to support herself from her own land. The inspector notes the detailed analysis in her application of potential productivity of the land- speaking to both the requirements for on-site food and also produce for sale in support of the "land-based business" element of an OPD. However, he then repeatedly damns this work- including recorded field trials of site-specific methods of cultivation with the comment

"the proposal would meet the requirements, provided the projections were considered to be realistic."

And in what way are the projections considered to be unrealistic?

"TAN6 says that OPD applications should be supported by robust evidence and a Management Plan produced by a "competent person", which I take to mean someone of relevant expertise who can make an independent assessment (though the term is not defined in TAN6). In this case, the Appellant has produced the Management Plan herself, and I cannot rely on the information in it unless it is backed by clear evidence to support the various assertions made."

Here we have in explicit terms the valorisation of one specific type of knowledge; that produced by expertise, academic and professional validation, privilege, at its core male dominated and dominating in practice over that produced by nurturing, co-operation, sharing, practical experience- at its core essentially a female form of competence, understanding and knowing the world and how to live well within it. That the remarks are a constructed negation is further revealed when simply comparing forms of words a few lines and sections apart where the inspector is able to simultaneously hold the views that;

"Some planting and growing has already taken place in 2018 and 2019, and the Appellant has used the results of these trials to help make projections of future production levels at the end of a 5-year period. She has compared these with the likely needs of the proposed occupants and argues that the requirements of the OPD Guidance would be met."

And…

"Appellant has produced the Management Plan herself, and I cannot rely on the information in it unless it is backed by clear evidence to support the various assertions made. In this respect the Management Plan is deficient in a number of elements."

The punch line here of course is that the applicant did not write the plan entirely alone, she was ably assisted by an acknowledged expert who, on the basis of previous experiences, elected not to include his own name and qualifications.

The report also calls into question Ms. D's estimates of the required hours for various types of work and phases of the development. I suggest that this type of judgmental remark also falls into that class of male devaluation of women's efforts, capacities and adaptability.

It also calls into question, as indeed do all of the responses to OPD business plans, who exactly is qualified to examine such plans and on what basis? Can a member of a local authority planning team, no doubt trained and qualified sufficient to their task, be expected to properly understand what is required to undertake a new business- indeed one on which the applicant's entire life and wellbeing- is critically dependent? Indeed, I suggest that the greater privilege of position and formal qualifications puts the inspectors at an even greater remove from the "all-in" risk being taken by the OPD applicants- thus rendering them even less capable of understanding the levels of committed effort being shown by OPD practitioners.

The lesson from this part of the analysis is more practical and applicable. New applicants would do well to ensure that every part of their plan relating to land use and productivity is supported by recognised (indeed reified) evidence. If not produced by men, then the work of women of exceptional expertise and qualifications will suffice. Where soils are typed as "poor" show precisely how you will overcome this. Where you have made trials, ensure you evidence these with recorded quantities and photographs. Where your business includes low density high added value goods such as crafts demonstrate sales and future diversification of products. Ideally have letters of intent from buyers in bulk.

In conclusion, and now in haste as there are more demanding tasks entering my work flow, I remain shocked at how Ms. D was treated by the LPA, her ward councillor, and PINS Wales. Clearly there is much within this case that could become the basis of legal action, but only if funds or pro bono support become available. From her starting position of Habermassian compliance, by making an application for an OPD to formalise her simple wish to support herself from her own efforts on her own land, Ms. D has discovered that in reality she lives in a Foucauldian world of state power and enforcement. In this world the work and knowledges of women continue to be negated ignored or at minimum devalued by the practitioners within the system of state control. I share this, and my interstitial "lessons" with anyone who cares as a caution, a reminder that however civil, reasonable and equitable our local governance systems may appear on the surface, achieving radical change requires exceptional attention to the Foucauldian reality of the powers embedded within the "Local State"11. This attention is the minimum requirement for an informed approach to using the TAN6 OPD policy in areas of Wales where the local powers are becoming increasingly hostile towards the policy and its practitioners.

Notes:

1. Decision http://planningdocs.pembrokeshire.gov.uk/NPSPublicDocs/00382615.pdf

2. For an insight into what TAN 6 OPD policy is start here and follow the links in the drop menus to more details.

http://www.oneplanetcouncil.org.uk/

3. For the documents relating to the second application.

http://planning.pembrokeshire.gov.uk/swiftlg/apas/run/WPHAPPDETAIL.DisplayUrl?theApnID=19/0190/PA&theTabNo=4&backURL=%3Ca%20href=wphappcriteria.display?paSearchKey=1233437%3ESearch%20Criteria%3C/a%3E%20%3E%20%3Ca%20href=%27wphappsearchres.displayResultsUR

4. Guy de Bord "The Society of the Spectacle" The text is widely available from many sources online but I recommend you support radical book distribution by purchasing a hard copy from Rebel Press; https://freedompress.org.uk/

5. For an introductory critical examination of the comparative positions of Habermas and Foucauld see this paper from Bernt Flyvberg

https://www.jstor.org/stable/591310?seq=1

6. Stating the obvious, this analysis is classical Marxist in origin.

7. The Practice Guidance notes are here

https://gov.wales/planning-permission-one-planet-developments-open-countryside

8. A good introduction to the ideas of Colin Ward is found in

https://www.akpress.org/autonomysolidaritypossibility.html

9. Fairlie; Simon. Low Impact Development, Planning and People in a Sustainable Countryside (2nd Edition) 2009. Jon Carter Publishing, Alder House, Charlebury, OX7 3PH

{There seem to be many copies of the 1st ed. available to buy online, but this 2nd ed. seems to have become unobtainable- perhaps time for a reprint ?}

10. For more about this see the work of Marion Shoard

http://www.marionshoard.co.uk/Books/This-Land-Is-Our-Land.php

11. For a good account of the transformation of council officers from public servants to technocratic managers see https://www.goodreads.com/book/show/2497235.The_Local_State

Afterword. As I don't get paid for any of this work, I do accept random donations via my paypal

pete@lifespacedesign.co.uk

And I do have a taste for matured single malts and non-chill filtered whiskies- including Penderyn.

Peace Out.

Pete Linnell   May 2020 in C19 lockdown.

Grow Your Own Home

www.gyoh.org.uk

Pete's appendices are free to share;

— Copy and redistribute the material in any medium or formatAdapt

— Remix, transform, and build upon the material for any purpose, even commercially.

Printed in Great Britain
by Amazon